Celebrate!

An Anti-Bias Guide to Enjoying Holidays

in Early Childhood Programs

Celebrate!

An Anti~Bias Guide to Enjoying Holidays

in Early Childhood Programs

Julie Bisson

with a preface by
LOUISE DERMAN~SPARKS

Redleaf Press
St. Paul, Minnesota
www.redleafpress.org

Published by Redleaf Press
a division of Resources for Child Caring
10 Yorkton Court
St. Paul, MN 55117
Visit us online at www.redleafpress.org.

Redleaf Press books are available at a special discount when purchased in bulk for special
premiums and sales promotions. For details, contact the sales manager at 800-423-8309.

Library of Congress Cataloging-in-Publication Data
Bisson, Julie, 1963–
    Celebrate! : an anti-bias guide to enjoying holidays in early
childhood programs / by Julie Bisson.
        p. cm.
    Includes bibliographical references.
    ISBN-10: 1-884834-32-9 (alk. paper)
    ISBN-13: 978-1-884834-32-5
    1. Holidays—Study and teaching (Early childhood)—United States.
2. Early childhood education—United States—Activity programs.
I. Title.
GT4803.A2B57 1997
372.83—dc21   97-23504
                                                              CIP

Manufactured in the United States of America

In memory of my grandmother,
Armida Coppola Rotondo,
who really loved to celebrate

Contents

Preface by Louise Derman-Sparks xi

Acknowledgments xv

Introduction: Why a Book About Holidays? xvii

   About This Book xviii

   Organization xix

   How to Use This Book xx

   A Message to You, the Reader xx

SECTION I: RETHINKING HOLIDAYS

Chapter 1: The Meanings of Holidays 1

   Personal Meanings 1

   Social Meanings 3

   Complexities and Different Perspectives 3

Chapter 2: Current Approaches and New Ideas 5

   Current Practices 5

   The Trap of the Tourist Approach 7

   The Value of Celebrating 9

   Benefits of a Holiday Curriculum 10

   New Ideas 10

SECTION II: PLANNING FOR CHANGE

Chapter 3: Assess Your Situation 15

   Understand Your Own Perspective 16

   What Filter Am I Using? 16

   Think About Your Position 16

   Evaluate Your Home/School Relationships 17

Improving Home/School Communication 19
Acknowledge the Challenges of Collaboration 20

Chapter 4: Develop a Holiday Policy 21
Include Everyone Who Wants to Be Included 22
Choose a Method 23
Set Your Own Ground Rules 24
Outline Your Policy 25
XYZ Child Care Center Holiday Policy 27
Periodically Evaluate Your Policy 31
Sample Holiday Evaluation Questionnaire for Families 32

Chapter 5: Determine Your Goals 35
Consider Possible Goals 35
Anti-Bias Curriculum Goals 36
Consult Your Program Goals 38
Think About the Children and Families in Your Setting 38
Reflect and Review 39

Chapter 6: Select Holidays 41
Gather Information From Families 42
Select Your Methods 42
Sample Family Questionnaire About Holidays 43
Support Reluctant Families 45
Points to Remember 45
Review Your Information About Families 46
Find Out About Program Requirements 46
Add Your Own Choices 47
Evaluate Your List 49

Chapter 7: Evaluate Holiday Activities 51
Meet to Review Your Activities 51
Plan for Improvement 52
Holiday Practices Improvement Plan 53

SECTION III: HOLIDAYS IN YOUR CLASSROOM

Chapter 8: Remembering Developmentally Appropriate Practice 57
Holiday Ages and Stages 58
Work With Children 59
Keep Holiday Activities in Check 61
Choose Appropriate Themes 64

Chapter 9: Reflecting All Children 69
Activities That Reflect Home 69
Culture Throughout Your Curriculum 70
Work Sensitively With Families 71
Create Balance 71
Avoid Balance Traps 73

Chapter 10: Introducing Unfamiliar Holidays 77

Consider Children's Development 78

Consider the Community Context 78

Diversity in Homogenous Groups 79

Use a Diagram to Help You Decide 80

Concentric Circles Diagrams 82

Strategies for Including Unfamiliar Holidays 84

Sample Persona Doll Story 85

Points to Remember 88

Chapter 11: Addressing Stereotypes and Commercialism 91

Understand Stereotypes 92

Address Holiday Stereotypes in Your Classroom 94

Talk With Families 95

Address Commercialism 96

Respond to Families' Circumstances 98

Help Children Stand Up to Bias 98

Chapter 12: Considering Religion 101

Consider Your Own Perspective 101

What Are Your Thoughts About Religion? 102

Monitor Your Responses 102

Identify Your Program Type 103

Consult Your Program's Philosophy 104

Reflect on Your Goals 104

Work With Families 105

When Families Disagree 105

Choose Your Approach 106

Points to Remember 109

Consider Issues of Diversity 110

Chapter 13: Meeting Needs When Families Don't Celebrate 111

Examine Your Own Feelings 112

Dialogue With Families 113

Provide Information 113

Ask Questions 114

Recheck Your Emotions 114

Provide Different Options 115

Communicate With Other Families 117

Support Children 117

Chapter 14: Michael's, Sheryl's, and Margery's Classrooms 121

Michael's Story 121

Sheryl's Story 126

Margery's Story 129

Conclusion: A Final Word 133

Resources 135

  Books for Children 135

  Birth Days and Rituals 136

  Columbus Day 136

  Rosh Hashanah 136

  Sukkot 136

  Halloween 137

  Diwali 137

  Dia de Los Muertos 137

  Thanksgiving/Being Thankful 138

  Solstice 138

  Hanukkah 138

  Christmas 139

  Christmas and Hanukkah 139

  Kwanzaa 139

  Chinese New Year 140

  Martin Luther King, Jr.'s Birthday 140

  Têt 141

  Valentine's Day 141

  Purim 141

  St. Patrick's Day 141

  Easter 142

  Passover 142

  Cinco de Mayo 142

  Kodomo-no-hi 143

  Ramadan 143

  Id ul-Fitr 143

  Potlatch 143

  Powwow 144

  Seasonal/Harvest 144

  General/Compilations 145

  Books About Similarities and Differences 146

  Adult Resources 146

  Books 146

    Holidays 146

    General Education 147

    Anti-Bias/Multicultural 147

    Religion 148

  Articles 148

Preface

by Louise Derman-Sparks

In my workshops and conversations about anti-bias education with early childhood practitioners throughout the country, the "holiday question" invariably comes up. The many-faceted issues connected to the topic are not only of intellectual interest; they also spark strong emotions that shape the conversations—even when the people involved are not aware this is happening.

Holidays matter deeply to people. They represent a host of experiences, feelings, connections, and memories of family and close friends; many of which are warm and positive, some of which are filled with anxiety, anger, or pain. Consequently, asking people to rethink how and why they have been using holiday activities in their early childhood programs is a much more complex and difficult task than it may first appear. It isn't surprising that considerable confusion characterizes where many teachers are on this volatile issue.

Moreover, certain basic misconceptions cloud the very necessary dialogue about the role holidays play in an anti-bias curriculum for young children. The most prevalent misconception is that an anti-bias approach means the elimination of all holidays from the curriculum. In fact, *Anti-Bias Curriculum: Tools for Empowering Young Children,* the book I wrote with the ABC Task Force, has an entire chapter devoted to a discussion about holidays. It *does not* say that people should stop all holiday activities in their educational program. It does raise many questions about how we have used holidays in the past as the focus of multicultural activities and about the ways we have presented and involved children in holiday activities. The primary message of the chapter about holidays is to encourage early childhood educators to rethink and make changes as necessary in their practice.

Unfortunately, instead of taking on the challenging—and possibly daunting—task of rethinking their practice, some people have opted for a "No Holiday" policy. This solution only causes further problems. It deprives children and families of a potentially enriching aspect of early childhood care and education; it deprives staff of the stretching and growing conversations essential to rethinking holiday policy and initiating new approaches. The "no-holiday" solution also results in some individuals unfairly holding the anti-bias approach responsible for policies that it neither suggests nor upholds.

Another source of confusion about holidays is the anti-bias book's critique of the form of multicultural curriculum we label the "tourist approach." As part of our criticism, we point to the *overuse* of holidays as the *primary strategy for introducing children to cultural diversity.* Because, by definition, holidays are special days in all people's culture, over-reliance on holiday activities results in children not learning about the daily life of people different from themselves and thus prevents them from understanding the diverse ways people live out their shared human needs. Incorporating holiday activities as *one* strategy for respecting and learning about human diversity is appropriate. However, using holidays *exclusively* to teach about diversity does become "tourist" curriculum!

The position the anti-bias book takes on so-called national holidays—that is, those treated in child care and school settings as equally meaningful for all American children—has also sparked considerable disequilibrium and, in some cases, hostility. Nevertheless, how to address holidays such as Thanksgiving, Christmas, Easter, or Mother's Day within an anti-bias perspective does require serious rethinking. Each of these holidays represents the cultural/religious way of life and view of history of a considerable part of the population of the U.S.A.—*but not of all.* Many people do not consider these holidays central to their cultural or religious group's way of life. Not all groups subscribe to the view of history as expressed, for example, in the traditional Thanksgiving story. Increasing numbers of families do not fit easily into the make-one-gift-for-mother tradition of Mother's Day.

This reality poses a core dilemma to educators who wish to create a democratic and inclusive early childhood program that nurtures all children in relation to their family context. How do we carry out our professional responsibility to authentically and sensitively include the cultural perspectives and life experiences of all the families whose children we serve, while also fostering all children's emotional, cognitive, and behavioral abilities to effectively and fairly interact with people different from themselves? Both responsibilities are essential to our nation's healthy survival. We can not disparage, ignore, or inaccurately reflect some groups in favor of others.

Yet, to some people, respectful inclusion of any other group's cultural or historic perspective in the curriculum is considered a denial of their own rights. In other words, to some, "If it is not my way, then I am being victimized." As a profession, we know how to productively work with the "egocentricism" of preschoolers who assume their views are shared by everyone else and who cry "not fair" when they want the bike someone else is riding at the time. We are not made anxious by having to do conflict resolution and problem-solving about sharing and taking turns with children—indeed we do this on a regular basis. But most have yet to effectively work with the conflicting and frequently ethnocentric views and needs of adults, whether they are our colleagues, staff, or the adult members of the families we serve.

Yet, this is exactly what we must learn how to do. *Celebrate! An Anti-Bias Guide to Enjoying Holidays in Early Childhood Programs* provides the tools for addressing the "holiday question" in new, creative, and effective ways. It does not solve the problems; rather it gives you strategies for solving them yourself in collaboration with staff and families. There is no one "Right Way" for incorporating holiday activities within an anti-bias approach. What is "right" or meaningful for the group of children and families you serve and the teachers who bring curriculum to life can only be decided collaboratively by the people involved. This book will help you do so if you have the courage, commitment, and persistence to make it happen.

Acknowledgments

No book would be complete without specific mention of the special and talented people that helped shape it. There are a multitude of people whom I want to thank for helping to make this book possible.

The idea for this book was conceived as I was collecting data for my master's degree at Pacific Oaks College in Pasadena, California. Parenthetical citations made in this book refer to my unpublished master's thesis. My deepest thanks to the following educators whose willingness to be interviewed and generosity with information helped to make this book what it is:

Cecelia Alvarado, Director, National Early Childhood Leadership Initiative, Wheelock College

ReGena Booze, Faculty, Pacific Oaks College

Phyllis Brady, Director of Student Diversity, Outreach, and Academic Enrichment, College of Engineering, University of California Santa Barbara

Sharon Cronin, Faculty, Pacific Oaks College Northwest

Louise Derman-Sparks, Faculty, Pacific Oaks College

Cory Gann, Practicum Supervisor, Central Washington University

Cheryl Greer, Faculty, Pacific Oaks College

Eric Hoffman, Master Teacher, Cabrillo College Children's Center

Roberta Hunter, Education Training Program Manager, Head Start

Katie Kissinger, Early Childhood Education Consultant

Norma Quan Ong, Resource Teacher, San Francisco Unified School District, Child Development Department

Deborah Owens, Associate Academic Dean, Pacific Oaks College

Patricia Ramsey, Professor of Psychology and Education and Director of Gorse Child Study Center, Mt. Holyoke College

xvi

★ ★
★ ★
★ ★

Celebrate!

B.J. Richards, Family Child Care Provider

Kim Sakamoto Steidl, Elementary School Teacher and College Instructor

Bill Sparks, Teacher Advisor, Intergroup Relations, Los Angeles Unified School District

Kay Taus, Director, Even Start Family Literacy Program

Stacey York, Instructor, Child Development Program, Minneapolis Community and Technical College

I am also indebted to the readers who graciously took the time to read this manuscript and give me invaluable feedback. They are ReGena Booze, Claire Chang, Sharon Cronin, Louise Derman-Sparks, Mary Pat Martin, Virginia Maldonado, and Stacey York.

To the staff, families, and children at Kidspace Child Care Center who participated in *so* many conversations about our holiday policy and effective holiday practices, especially Michelle Bretz, Amy Carrigan, Jenifer Del Grande, Helen Froissart, Beth Goss, and Lorena Kidd. Thank you for allowing me to practice on you and for teaching me so much about what it means to implement practices in the real world.

To my editor, Ilene Rosen...you are more like the co-author of this book than the editor. I appreciate tremendously the time, energy, and skill that you put into this project. You helped to mold and shape this book and turn it into what it is. Thank you, too, to Mary Steiner Whelan, the Managing Editor of Redleaf Press, for thinking this book was a good idea and encouraging me along the way.

Thank you to my family for never doubting that I could write this book and for being my biggest fans.

Gracias to my "second best" friend Linda Irene Jimenez. Our nightly talks and your regular words of encouragement went a long way.

Thank you, Louise, for all the reasons that you are aware of. Your mentoring and friendship will be forever precious to me.

And last but not least, thank you to Jeff, for understanding every time I had to turn down an invitation to go skiing, hiking, snow shoeing, or camping due to the demands of this book.

Why a Book About Holidays?

I have always loved holidays. When I was growing up, holidays were times of anticipation, festive feelings, warmth, and family togetherness.

As an early childhood educator, I carried my love of holidays into the classroom, wanting to re-create with the children what I had enjoyed with my family. It wasn't until I was teaching in the child care program at Pacific Oaks Children's School in Pasadena, California, and learning about anti-bias education that I began to feel uneasy about how I was approaching holidays in the classroom. As a staff, we put a lot of time and energy into researching holidays, but I began to doubt that children were gaining what I had hoped from the activities. They didn't always seem to be connecting to the underlying meaning of the holiday. In some cases, the holidays and their corresponding activities seemed too far removed from the children's own experiences to be meaningful. While my goal for many of the holiday activities was to help the children learn more about the people who celebrated them, I suspect that sometimes the children saw these people as "too different." They weren't able to see the parallels between themselves and the people whose holidays we were celebrating.

As I talked to other teachers and to teacher trainers, I discovered I wasn't the only one who had questions and concerns about holidays. This curriculum component had many of my colleagues and mentors feeling frustrated, confused, and overwhelmed.

Celebrate!

My observations about holidays prompted me to research this topic for my master's thesis. I began by interviewing a multiethnic group of eighteen educators who are knowledgeable about both early childhood education and culturally relevant, anti-bias education. I asked them a series of questions about how holidays might be incorporated into an early childhood program using an anti-bias approach. The results of those interviews profoundly impacted my thinking about holidays and continue to affect my work in this area.

Over the last six years I've presented many workshops on holidays and consulted with private and public early childhood programs as they made their own decisions about how to handle holidays. I have also struggled with this issue myself, as a director of a private, nonprofit child care program serving children aged two months through five years. These experiences continually remind me of the many different facets of holiday practices and the complexity of the challenges as well as the solutions.

About This Book

If you are a teacher, director, or supervisor in an early childhood program and are considering changing your approach to holidays, this book was written for you. It will also be useful to you if you are a teacher-trainer interested in helping teachers think about holidays in new ways. Holidays in the classroom are an area of much debate and struggle. Many teachers are grappling with this curriculum component. How to make holiday activities meaningful for children, how to relate them to their families, and how to implement activities accurately and respectfully are some of the many hurdles teachers face. Addressing diversity, avoiding stereotypes, handling the religious aspects of holidays, and meeting the needs of families who do not celebrate are others.

If you and I were sitting in a room and talking, instead of you reading these words on a page, I'd ask you what you hope to get from this book. Perhaps you are looking through it because you are uncomfortable with your current approach to holidays and are not sure how to change it. Possibly your program or classroom presently has a policy of not celebrating holidays because of the difficulty in doing them well, and you would prefer to find ways to include holidays using a more effective approach. Or maybe you are reading this book to find ideas for celebrating specific holidays, like Kwanzaa.

While you will find ideas in these pages for celebrating holidays, you should know that this is *not* a holiday activity book. Instead, this book attempts to create a framework of things to consider about how to create holiday activities that are enjoyable for children, and are also in tune with the anti-bias approach that includes being meaningful, culturally appropriate, and inclusive. It is meant to be a guide as you answer your own questions about how to handle holidays in your setting.

Organization

This book is organized into three sections. The first section, "Rethinking Holidays," will help you understand the important issues involved in holidays themselves (chapter 1) and in implementing them in early childhood classrooms (chapter 2). Chapter 2 also describes in broad terms what a good, anti-bias approach to holidays should include.

The second section, "Planning for Change," guides you through the steps of changing your approach to holidays. Chapter 3, "Assess Your Situation," will help you examine your own feelings, your position, and your relationships with the families you work with. It also discusses how to collaborate with families and colleagues, a necessary part of the process. Chapter 4, "Develop a Holiday Policy," suggests ways to formalize your approach into a written policy as you make choices and implement changes. Chapters 5 and 6 will guide you through making important decisions about your goals for holiday activities (chapter 5) and which holidays to include in your classroom to help you meet those goals (chapter 6). Evaluating is an important part of the process of change. Chapter 7 offers tools to help you review and plan to improve your activities as you move forward.

The third section, "Holidays in Your Classroom," is full of steps and strategies that will help you successfully implement holiday activities in your classroom. There are many issues to address. Chapter 8 offers information about making sure your curriculum is developmentally appropriate, a basic but sometimes overlooked aspect of holiday activities. Chapter 9 explains how and why your activities need to reflect the home practices of all the children in your group. Chapter 10 addresses a key question teachers have about holidays as they relate to an anti-bias/multicultural curriculum: When, if ever, is it appropriate to introduce a holiday into your curriculum that no one in your group celebrates? If it is, how should it be done? Chapter 11 talks about addressing stereotypes and commercialism, two unfortunate aspects of some holidays, which, nevertheless, provide opportunities for critical thinking and working to counter bias. Religion is an important piece of many holidays. Chapter 12 offers information to help you decide how to address this topic sensitively and appropriately for your particular children and setting. Chapter 13 explains why some families don't want their children to participate in some or any holiday activities, and how you can effectively meet the needs of everyone in your group when that happens. Chapter 14 provides windows into three different classrooms that use successful anti-bias approaches to holidays. This chapter lets you see some of the many ways that the strategies and suggestions in this book can be put into action.

The book ends with a list of resources that will give you an idea of the wealth of holiday resources available. Complete references for all the sources quoted throughout the book are also here. The list of children's books is a partial list of good children's literature that is available about holidays. Use the books that tell stories about the holidays you include in your curriculum. The list also includes adult resources, articles, and books that you can use to get more information and ideas about the topic of holidays.

How to Use This Book

Throughout this book, you will find ideas and suggestions about working with families, which is a critical part of planning and implementing an inclusive, sensitive holiday program. For ease of reading, the book will generally refer to parents and guardians or families when referring to any adults who care for and care about a child in your program, including grandparents, partners or companions, legal guardians, and other important adults in children's lives.

This book is organized in sequential fashion to help you go about the process of reflecting on and changing your approach to holidays. You might find it useful to start at the beginning and read each chapter in order. If you don't plan to read the entire book from start to finish, and you are the kind of person who likes to jump into action, start with the second section. It will refer you to other places in the book to find the information you need as you go along. On the other hand, if you prefer to get all the information before you act, you might like to start with the third section. The first section includes important information that you should read before you actually implement changes in your program, but it doesn't have to be read before the other sections of the book.

A Message to You, the Reader

As you work through this book and through your own efforts to provide a more effective holiday curriculum, it may help you to think of the process as a journey, one that will continue for a long time to come. I welcome you on that journey.

For me, it has been somewhat like going through an old trunk of my grandmother's that I found in the attic. As I pulled off the top layer of clothes and memoirs, I felt overwhelmed with feelings and responsibilities. I worked through those issues and then dug deeper, only to find more surprises and challenges. The process continued with intermittent joy, sadness, regret, and relief. I finally got to the bottom of the trunk, but I often revisit the items that I found buried underneath one another.

I suspect that you too will make some mistakes on your journey, and you will have some tremendous successes. This is hard work. Holidays have been a focal point of early childhood curriculum for many years, and old habits are hard to break. And since holidays can be very personal and emotional, you will probably encounter some strong emotions and possibly some resistance as you go foreword on your journey. Don't give up! Change may be slow, but that's okay. Take baby steps. Every small move forward is an accomplishment. As you endeavor through your journey, remember: The thought and effort you put in will make you a more effective teacher and create a more responsive environment for your children.

I also want you, the reader, to know that I am a European American woman. I identify strongly with my Italian American heritage. I grew up on the East Coast and have spent the last eleven years on the West Coast. Like any writer, my identity and my life experiences have shaped what I have written on these pages.

My intent in this book is to offer you guideposts for your journey, not to tell you exactly how to handle holidays. I hope that you'll find this information useful as you make your own decisions about how to approach holidays in your program.

Good luck!

RETHINKING HOLIDAYS

CHAPTER **1**

The Meanings of Holidays

Holidays in early childhood classrooms often mean art activities, special foods, and fun. But in the world outside, holidays can have a more profound meaning. They bring together experiences that touch the core of many people's lives, including family, friends, values, and religion. Before you can find new answers for handling holidays in your classroom, it helps to step back and look at what holidays are and why they can be so significant to the people who celebrate them.

Personal Meanings

For many of us, the pressure of busy, fast-paced lives has created a whirling, twirling, demanding day-to-day existence. In the whirlwind, we sometimes feel that we've lost sight of who we are, and we search for help in making meaning or making sense out of our lives again. Holiday rituals and celebrations can help to remind us who we are and what is really important.

Because holidays have become so influenced by the media—magazines tell us how to cook, decorate, and dress, and television shows and videos portray perfect holiday dinners that we feel we should replicate—we may have to clear away all the of commercialism to uncover the true meanings and values inherent in holidays. It is possible to accomplish this.

Celebrate!

Think about your own current experiences with holidays. Is there one that is particularly special to you as an adult, one that you really enjoy celebrating? Consider why that holiday is important to you. What about it is so special? What feelings does the celebration bring up for you? The answers to these questions reveal some of the meanings that holidays hold for you personally.

Not all adults enjoy holidays. But those who do name the same reasons why they are meaningful time and time again. Here are a few examples.

Family/Friend connectedness

Holidays are a time for gathering. People often have fond childhood memories of getting together with extended family around a particular holiday, talking, laughing, playing or otherwise enjoying one another. They may continue this tradition as adults with family, or use the opportunity for special gatherings with friends instead.

Magic

The rituals of preparing for some holidays—cooking, decorating, shopping, traveling, even cleaning—can bring up wonderful feelings of warmth, excitement, and anticipation. These feelings often begin before the holiday starts and may linger long after.

Rhythm of life

When holidays come around each year, they remind people of the rhythmic passing of seasons and time. Repeating the same holiday traditions can bring a sense of security, familiarity, and predictability to our ever-changing world.

Connection to cultural roots

Many holiday traditions are closely tied to the cultures that our parents and grandparents came from. Participating in cultural traditions helps people to feel closer to their backgrounds and their ancestors. These connections can be particularly meaningful when they are reminders of relatives who have passed away.

Spirituality and values

Spirituality which can be reaffirmed or renewed each year plays a large role in holidays for many of us. Going to our place of worship, singing special songs, recounting historical and/or religious stories, and eating significant foods can all reinforce beliefs about the world.

Holidays also symbolize or remind us of the values and meaningful principles that sometimes get lost in everyday life. Values that many of us hold, such as love, care, joy of life, sense of wonder, awe, trust, thankfulness, and hope, are evident in the meanings and rituals that underlie many holidays. Holidays also provide us with a chance to assess and reflect on our lives and set goals for the future.

Social Meanings

In addition to personal meaning, most holidays include deep-seated religious, cultural, or historical perspectives. For example, many people in the United States celebrate the Fourth of July to remember and celebrate the day when the United States became free. It is a cultural and historical event. For many Mexican people, Dia de Los Muertos is a religious holiday and a cultural event. On this day family members and friends get together to remember their loved ones who have passed away. For many individuals in different cultural groups, Easter is a religious holiday that celebrates the resurrection of Jesus Christ after his death on the cross.

Holidays serve the needs of the individuals and groups who celebrate them. They teach the values of a particular group and a particular version of history, and often reinforce relationships to a chosen deity. Holidays and their rituals serve as reminders to adults and teach young people what the group considers important.

Complexities and Different Perspectives

Because of our diverse histories and cultures, the same holiday can have various meanings to people of different religious or cultural groups. Sometimes, the same holiday can be understood and celebrated in different, almost opposite ways.

Thanksgiving is one example. For many families, Thanksgiving is a happy, warm holiday about togetherness and giving thanks for food and other blessings. It also celebrates a shared perspective on history, featuring a story about goodwill and friendship. However, to some people, especially those who are Native American, Thanksgiving can be a reminder of many years of unfairness and hurt. It marks the beginning of a devastating time in history when promises were broken, possessions were stolen, and families were separated and killed. The feeling is so strong among Native Americans that many have begun to recognize it as a day of mourning.

For many European Americans, Columbus Day is a day to remember a courageous explorer who helped pave the way for Europeans to come to this country. In contrast, individuals in some Latin communities celebrate Columbus Day as Dia de La Raza, which commemorates the survival of people over the five hundred years since Columbus' "invasion" of the Americas.

Christmas is celebrated as a national holiday. Businesses, schools, banks, governmental agencies, and most retail stores are closed. However, Christmas is a religious holiday. For Christians, the Christmas season can be a joyous time that creates opportunities for connection with others and celebrates shared

Celebrate!

religious beliefs. However, for many people in the United States who aren't Christian, the emphasis on this day can feel ostracizing.

Here's another perspective. There are many people living in the United States who do not celebrate holidays at all. Our society's emphasis on holidays, particularly those that fall from October through December, can cause difficulties for them, and especially for their children.

All of these different perspectives impact on the children, families, and activities in your program. Whether your group is diverse or relatively homogeneous, there will be differences in the ways they celebrate and in the celebrations they see in our diverse society.

By now you can see that holidays are intensely felt, significant occasions for many people, perhaps including you and/or some of the children, families, and colleagues you work with. Perhaps that is why addressing holidays in early childhood classrooms can be so difficult.

CHAPTER **2**

Current Approaches and New Ideas

If the parents or guardians of a child walked into your classroom when your group was doing holiday activities, what do you think they would think about the holiday experiences you create in your classroom? Would the parents or guardians see children connected by feelings of warmth, validation, and community? Would they learn a little about the underlying meaning of the holiday? Would they see children involved in activities that they were comfortable with? Could they tell that the activities reflected the home lives of the children in the group?

Perhaps they would not. The fact is that in many programs across the country, holidays are not treated with the sensitivity and forethought they require. Instead, teachers use them freely as a primary method for organizing the year's curriculum, without realizing the negative impact that results when holidays are used inappropriately.

Current Practices

The following reasons help to explain why holiday curriculum in early childhood classrooms has come to be what it is.

Celebrate!

Holidays by habit

Sometimes early childhood educators, like everyone, get caught in a groove. When we discover something that works, we often keep doing the same thing, year after year. However, we may be doing something because we've always done it, without stopping to reevaluate whether or not our practices are appropriate to the children we are currently working with, or fit with the best thinking about developmentally appropriate teaching. This is sometimes the case with holidays in early childhood programs.

Reliance on packaged curriculum guides

Many early childhood educators entered the field in a trial by fire sort of way. We are hired and, often times without much orientation or training, put in a classroom with ten or twenty children and expected to go to work. Because we are educators and care about children, we do the best we can with what is available. For some teachers that means turning to curriculum guide books for ideas. But unfortunately, much of what is available through month-by-month, one-way-fits-all curriculum guides is not reflective of our children's lives and, sometimes, inappropriate and even hurtful to the children and families in our programs.

Frequently guide books are organized around holidays. You can turn to many curriculum books and see the same general format. Here is one example:

September	"I'm Me, I'm Special"
October	Halloween
November	Fall, Harvest, Thanksgiving
December	Winter, Christmas, Hanukkah
January	Community helpers or Transportation
February	Valentine's Day (sometimes with community helpers, especially mail carriers)
March	Spring
April	More Spring, Easter
May	More Spring, Weather, Memorial Day

When the source for classroom activities comes out of a commercial curriculum guide, we're often at risk of providing activities that are meaningless to the children we teach, since the activities do not emerge from their experiences, interests, or questions. In addition, relying on holiday-based curriculum can mean neglecting other important and meaningful activities for children.

An attempt to be multicultural

Early childhood educators know that it's important and valuable to celebrate cultural diversity in the classroom, and we seek out available resources for ideas about how to do that. Much of what we find are curriculum books that focus on celebrating the holidays of various cultures with the purpose of introducing and "doing" a multicultural curriculum. As a result, using holidays as a method for teaching about culture and celebrating diversity has become very popular. This practice in many ways even seems logical, especially since holidays already play an important role in the curriculum in many programs.

However, when holidays become the main or sole way to teach about cultural diversity, teachers do a grave injustice to children's education. Culture is not easily taught through simple activities. People learn about their own cultures from birth, through daily life. They learn about others' over time, by getting to know the people of that culture and how they live their daily lives. Since holidays are unique times during the year when business as usual comes to a halt, children can not learn about the usual, everyday routines of a cultural group by only learning about their holidays.

The Trap of the Tourist Approach

In *Anti-Bias Curriculum,* Louise Derman-Sparks and the ABC Task Force call the attempt to teach about a culture through holiday activities a "tourist curriculum," because children visit a culture, participate in a few isolated activities as one might do on vacation in another country, then return home to "regular" classroom life. Often times any images of the people who celebrate the holiday are absent from the classroom until the next year, when the holiday rolls around again.

Focusing primarily or solely on holidays to teach about different cultures runs the risk of several serious problems. They are

- trivializing a cultural group by implying that the only important thing about the group is a holiday and that the people in this group only dress up, sing, dance, and eat special foods

- promoting misinformation about a cultural group by disconnecting the meaning of the holiday from the context of their daily life

- misusing symbols or activities of a culture, some of which are meant only for members of the cultural group (i.e. sand painting and feather headdresses in Native American culture)

- stereotyping by implying that all members of a group celebrate in the exact same way

Here is an example of the problems presented by teaching culture through holidays. Cinco de Mayo (The Fifth of May) is a holiday, suggested in many holiday curriculum books, about a victory for Mexican people. It honors Mexico becoming free from French rule. This victory was inspirational to many people fighting for Mexican independence, although it was not the most important battle in many years of struggle. Some people in Mexico and in the United States celebrate this holiday to commemorate Mexico's victory in battle.

But in early childhood programs, Cinco de Mayo is often used as an opportunity to teach about people who are Mexican and Mexican American. Some common activities used to celebrate this holiday include making a piñata; making tortillas; eating burritos for lunch; using serapes, sombreros, and Mexican cooking utensils in the dramatic play area; counting in Spanish; and learning a Mexican hat dance. The underlying reason for the holiday is not taught.

Thus the meaning of the holiday, as well as a true understanding of the diversity of Mexican and Mexican American people, is lost in these kinds of "celebrations." The activities teach nothing about the daily lives of Mexican American people and how they go about working, learning, playing, or loving their families. Such activities neglect the many connections and similarities between Mexican American children and American children of other ethnic backgrounds, and focus instead on minor differences.

What children may learn instead by participating only in these activities is that all Mexican and Mexican American people celebrate Cinco de Mayo (which is not true), that all Mexican and Mexican American people wear serapes and sombreros (also not true), and that the important things about

Mexicans and Mexican Americans is that they celebrate Cinco de Mayo, eat burritos, and play with piñatas (clearly not true).

In addition, this approach to learning about Cinco de Mayo overlooks the vast differences among the lives of people who live in different parts of Mexico and the differences between Mexican people living there, and Mexican American people living in the United States. These prevalent Cinco de Mayo activities can be hurtful and confusing to Mexican and Mexican American children, as well as to their classmates, if their lives don't match the holiday descriptions of "what Mexicans do."

The Value of Celebrating

By now you might be wondering what the alternatives are to these current approaches to holidays, and maybe even thinking that the problems of holidays are too complex to solve in your classroom. In that case, the best course might seem to be omitting holidays entirely from your curriculum.

In fact, some teachers have decided, for many reasons, to have a "No Holiday" policy. This is a viable option that makes sense for some programs; for example, a program where children are too young or not able cognitively to understand much about holiday activities, or if many families in a program are opposed to classroom holiday celebrations for religious reasons.

However, in most programs, leaving holidays completely out of children's classroom experiences can have negative consequences, especially for those children whose holidays are not typically reflected in dominant society. If you are a child (or adult) whose holiday is never reflected in stores, in television programming, on holiday cards, in the movies, in decorations, and so on, having your holiday omitted from your early childhood program as well can be painful (Sharon Cronin, 1992). Also, if you don't include holidays in your program, you are leaving out an important part of families' lives.

Furthermore, including holidays in your curriculum offers a variety of positive points, in addition to challenges. The following table offers a list of the benefits that thoughtfully planned holiday activities can bring. The list was developed by a group of families and staff members at a private, nonsectarian child care program.

Celebrate!

Benefits of a Holiday Curriculum

- Demonstrates that different beliefs are good
- Respects diversity
- Validates a child's and family's experiences
- Connects children's lives at home and school
- Provides a way for children and teachers to get to know each other on another level
- Is fun
- Breaks up the routine
- Celebrates positive things
- Instills values
- Enriches the children's experiences
- Provides opportunities for a child to feel special if he or she is the only one in the group who celebrates a holiday
- Allows for thoughtful dialogue between staff and families

New Ideas

If there are significant problems with many of the current approaches to holidays, what characterizes a good holiday curriculum?

Culturally relevant

As early childhood educators, we know that a good, effective program is individualized and meets children where they are developmentally. We also know that it is important to follow a child's lead, tuning in to who they are and basing curriculum and our interactions on their needs.

Many educators are also aware that culture is a large part of who children are. Everything they do is effected by culture, including the way they talk; how they dress; how they eat their food; where, when, and how they go to sleep; what games they play with friends; how far away they stand when talking to someone; how they are disciplined; and all other activities, interactions, and practices. Culture is also a part of holidays. What is celebrated by children and their families, how they celebrate, when, and with whom are all influenced by culture.

In essence, culture is a part of everything all human beings do. Even though it may be hard to see or difficult to define, it is there. When children are in situations that are culturally familiar and consistent with their own experiences, they feel more comfortable and secure. In these situations they can expect and predict that certain things will happen in particular ways.

All components of the early childhood program must be culturally relevant for children and families. When children walk through the classroom door every day, they should find elements of the room that look, smell, and feel familiar to them. This standard holds true for all components of the curriculum, including holiday activities. That means activities must reflect *what* is celebrated at home and *how* it is done. When this is accomplished, holiday activities are connecting, empowering, and validating for children.

Here is an example of the power of including culturally relevant holidays and activities in the program. A preschool program in Southern California enrolled children of different backgrounds. One year the teacher, ReGena, became aware that one family's cultural background was Persian (Iranian). When the mother came in on the first day of school to drop off her child, ReGena approached her and asked if her family celebrated Now-Ruz (Iranian New Year). The mother replied by grabbing ReGena's arm and exclaiming, "Oh, I will like it here! No one has ever asked me that before!" The mother's surprise and delight in ReGena's knowledge about her culture and in the idea of including this holiday in her child's program helped her to feel connected, safe, and comfortable in the school environment. Later, ReGena went to her book collection and pulled out information about Now-Ruz and other Iranian holidays and asked the mother if the information accurately reflected what their family believed and participated in. When the holiday arrived in March, the mother came in and participated in activities in the classroom with the children. The familiar holiday activities, along with other culturally relevant discussions and materials that ReGena included in the program, affected her and the child's comfort and identification with the classroom. Since the interactions, environment, and activities were culturally relevant, this child and her family thrived in the program (ReGena Booze, 1992).

Anti-Bias

In addition to reflecting individual children's cultural lives, an effective approach to holidays also advocates anti-bias goals, including helping children feel good about themselves, and teaching about and valuing similarities and differences.

Holiday activities can be one more way that teachers help children feel validated for who they are and what they do at home with their families. Whether or not children see themselves reflected around them is one of the ways they get messages about their value and worth. By seeing holidays and corresponding activities in the curriculum that are special to children and their families, children get a message that who they are and what is important to them is valuable to the teachers and others at school.

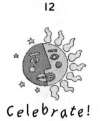

Celebrate!

Participating in activities and discussions about holidays that other children celebrate is one more way that children can learn about the similarities and differences between themselves and others. For example, during one December, a preschool-aged child in a child care center said to his teacher, "I celebrate Hanukkah. Abby celebrates Christmas. We both celebrate!"

Discussions about fairness and changing things that hurt people, two other anti-bias goals, can also emerge from holiday discussions in the classroom. Young children know a lot about "fair" and are eager to rectify unjust situations. Because some holiday decorations, stories, and messages negatively impact children's self-esteem and their growing ideas about who others are, involving children in activities that address the stereotypes and bias in holidays is a necessary and appropriate approach.

Developmentally appropriate

Teachers who create effective holiday programs are meticulous about considering children's developmental stages and daily experiences when planning activities. Teachers keep in mind each individual child and her or his development before deciding to include a holiday in the curriculum, when deciding how much and what kind of information to give children, when planning specific activities, and while answering children's questions.

The characteristics of good holiday curriculum outlined here are very different from the pre-packaged holiday curricula available in many books. Perhaps your own program lies somewhere in between. The remainder of this book will help you move from a less effective approach to holidays to an approach that is more relevant, meaningful, and appropriate to the children in your program.

PLANNING FOR CHANGE

CHAPTER **3**

Assess Your Situation

As you begin thinking about changing your approach to holidays, it's important to understand that this is an emotional issue. Holidays are a very meaningful and personal part of many people's lives, possibly even your own. If you feel strongly about holidays for religious or other personal reasons, it may be more emotionally challenging for you to look at holidays in new ways. Similarly, as an educator, you may have devoted a great deal of time, energy, and passion to the holiday curriculum you've been using and are now being asked to change. If this is the case, you may naturally have feelings of defensiveness or resistance that will take effort to overcome.

A second point to recognize when getting ready to change your approach is that you can't do this alone. Teachers, directors or supervisors, and the parents and guardians of the children must all work together in order to make significant, lasting changes.

This chapter will help you assess yourself and your setting in terms of these issues, so you can better understand where you are starting from as you begin to plan for change.

Celebrate!

Understand Your Own Perspective

Self-awareness is important. Whether or not you have strong personal feelings, it's important for you to know what perspective you are coming from when you approach the topic of holidays. Knowing your values, beliefs, feelings, and possible biases before you get started will make it easier for you to evaluate your current practices and consider new approaches that will better meet the needs of the children and families you are working with. The following questionnaire will help you clarify the thoughts and feelings you bring to this issue. Once you uncover your own perspective, keep it in mind as you sift through the information and suggestions offered in this book.

What Filter Am I Using?

Ask yourself these questions to help examine your own perspective:

- Did your family celebrate holidays when you were a child?
- How important were holidays to your family when you were growing up? How enjoyable were they?
- Which were your favorites?
- As a child in school, did you feel the holidays that were important to you and your family were respected? validated? considered "normal"?
- Did your family celebrate holidays the way you saw them portrayed in the media? Did you feel like you fit into that picture?
- Did you ever feel excluded either literally or figuratively because of what your family celebrated or didn't celebrate?
- How important are holidays to you in your adult life? Are there any that are particularly important to you? Any that you really enjoy or really don't like? Or do you avoid holidays all together?
- What do you really like about holidays? What do you dislike about them?
- Are any holidays you celebrate as an adult a part of your religious beliefs? If so, which ones? How do they relate to your religion?
- As an educator, how much of your current curriculum is devoted to holidays? How attached are you to the holidays and activities you have used in the past?

Think About Your Position

There are many players to consider as you go forward. Making successful changes in the way you approach holidays depends upon you, your co-workers, your supervisor, staff, and the children and families in your setting. It's important for everyone to work together. Without an agreement and everyone's support, your attempts to make changes and create consistency will be difficult.

Still, exactly who you involve and their degree of involvement depends on your position and the type of program you work in.

If you are a head or lead teacher in your classroom, you may have a certain amount of control over your curriculum and how you and your co-teachers approach holidays. It is important to gain the support of your director or supervisor and to work closely with co-workers or assistant teachers in your classroom to get their opinions and ideas.

If you are an assistant teacher, speak to your supervising teacher and your director or supervisor using the approach that works best for you. Let them know you would like to make changes in the way you approach holidays in the classroom. Tell them why. You will need to gain the interest of your supervising teacher, and co-workers if applicable, before going further.

If you are unable to gain the interest or support of your co-workers or supervisor, don't give up. You may not be able to make a sweeping change, but you can still change and improve the ways you talk to children about holidays and how you implement activities that you have control over. Keep a dialogue going with your colleagues at your center or school. Look for support and ideas from outside sources, too, such as community colleges that offer anti-bias courses, your local Association for the Education of Young Children (AEYC), or a support group of other educators who want to make change in this area.

If you are the director or educational supervisor, you probably have the greatest potential for making change in how holidays are approached in your program's classrooms. Since you might have a lot of control over your educational program, it may be possible for you to initiate change in the holiday curriculum in your setting. Start by sharing information—an article, a book, a conversation with a colleague, or a workshop you attended—about the value in rethinking your holiday program. Ask for input from your staff and families and encourage them to explore this with you further. Then, once the process is begun, your involvement and your support will remain essential. Teachers need to rely on you for ideas about educating others, gaining information from families, strategies for activities, and organizing staff or family meetings.

Evaluate Your Home/School Relationships

Whatever your position, children's families will be an integral part of the process as well. Parents and guardians have critical information that you will need in order to select and implement inclusive, culturally relevant holiday activities. In addition, they deserve communication about how their children may be affected by changes in holiday curriculum, and you will need their support

Celebrate!

in order to successfully put your changes into place. In fact, for many programs the best way to plan for change is to involve interested family members as partners who participate fully in the process of creating a new approach to holidays. (See the next chapter, "Developing a Holiday Policy.")

However, if you haven't already established an effective method of communication, asking for information and feedback about holidays may not be the place to start. The topic of holiday inclusion and implementation can be emotionally charged for families, as well as for teachers. Before you can approach this issue, it's necessary to look at your relationships with the families of the children in your care. To help you evaluate, ask yourself the questions below.

- How well do you communicate with families?

- When do you communicate with them? Do you see them every morning or every afternoon? Do you always talk with them for a few minutes about their child's day?

- What do you feel comfortable talking about with your families? Can you talk about toilet training, biting in the classroom, tips for handling sleeping or disciplining at home, and so on?

- Do you cross paths with parents and guardians outside of school? Are you comfortable talking with them informally on these occasions?

- Overall, how successful have your interactions with parents and guardians been?

If your ongoing communications with families are not as good as you would like, spend some time working to improve them. Choose a few of the strategies suggested on the following page and try them out for a month or two. Then, once you feel your communication is sound enough, you can begin to ask about holidays.

On the other hand, if you feel that you already have a good working relationship with your families, jump in! It's not necessary to strive for a perfect relationship before asking parents or guardians to become involved in the holiday planning process. But you do need to have a foundation so that asking about holidays won't seem out of place or alarming.

Improving Home/School Communication

Select the strategies that work best for you and your program.

Strive toward daily conversations. Try talking a little with all parents or guardians at drop-off or pick-up time. Share a bit about how each child's day was and what activities were available.

Use a communication notebook. If you don't have a chance to see families during the day, try putting out a notebook near the sign-in sheet. Parents and guardians can use this spot to leave you notes about their child or to ask questions they need answered. You can respond to their requests by calling them during the day or leaving a note in their mailbox or their child's cubby.

Consider making a family communication bulletin board. Hang a bulletin board in the classroom or just outside. Use it for posting newsletters, the teacher's names and the hours they work, your curriculum, articles about parenting, a wish list of materials for families to donate, etc.

Have a call-in time. Another strategy for keeping in touch with families and communicating the message that you want to know what's on their minds is to set aside a certain period of time (perhaps nap time or your planning time) when they can call you at the center with their questions or concerns.

Hold conferences. If you don't already, begin holding yearly or twice-yearly conferences to talk with families about their child's developmental progress and how the child spends his or her days in your program.

Spend time in the community. Participate in everyday activities in the neighborhoods where the children and families live. Shop at a local store, visit a park, eat at a restaurant, or go to the post office. Making this effort will go a long way to building strong, trusting relationships.

Celebrate!

Acknowledge the Challenges of Collaboration

Working together with colleagues and families is a necessary and valuable process in the effort to change your approach to holidays, but it is also a difficult one. As you begin to make decisions cooperatively, proceed with patience and thoughtfulness. Realize that this is indeed a process and that sometimes you may feel like you're taking two steps back for every step forward. But like any process, the most important thing is to keep on working, to keep your eyes on your goal. The following are some tips and reminders to help you stay on course.

▶ Strive to separate your personal holiday needs from the needs of the children in your classroom.

▶ It is okay to disagree. The important thing is to open up dialogue and listen to each other with respect and understanding.

▶ Keep checking in with yourself about your own feelings, values, and perspectives. This will help you keep your own opinions in view while remaining open to other ideas as well.

▶ Always remember that discussions about holidays may evoke strong emotional reactions. Expect to discuss the same issues several times so everyone has a chance to reflect, sort out their thoughts, and come to a consensus. Be patient.

▶ Finally, enjoy the process! Take advantage of the opportunities that arise to engage your co-workers and others in meaningful dialogue and the sharing of ideas.

CHAPTER 4

Develop a Holiday Policy

Formulating a holiday policy at the same time that you shape your new approach to holidays will help to make your decisions easier in the future. A holiday policy is a guide for everyone involved in your program to help them choose, implement, and evaluate holiday activities. The policy must be clear, detailed, and flexible. If you are a classroom teacher, it may be applicable to your individual room only. If you are a director or supervisor, your policy might guide your whole program.

Once you put your policy in place, you will always have it to refer to, to help guide your decisions as different situations arise. The policy can also be used to communicate your holiday approach to new staff and families who enter the program, but they also need to know that they can participate in improving and transforming the policy on an ongoing basis.

Many factors will play a role in determining when and how your policy is developed. You might want to begin developing it as you read through the chapters of this book. Or you might be more comfortable waiting until you've planned and implemented some holiday activities using a new approach, so you will have a sense of what works for you.

Celebrate!

It may work best for you to build your policy in stages. Try starting with reviewing your past holiday practices. Then develop agreed-upon goals to guide you in changing or improving your approach. Next, talk about how you will make decisions about which holidays to include. Last, give yourself time to work out the nitty-gritty issues of implementation. The rest of this book is set up to guide you through this process and offer information to help you make decisions.

Whatever approach you choose, remember that developing a holiday policy requires time and effort and will be affected by the successes and failures you experience in your classroom with each passing holiday. Don't be discouraged if it takes three meetings just to make one important decision, or if a whole year passes before you get your policy in writing.

Include Everyone Who Wants to Be Included

All teachers, assistants, and supervisors who will be affected by the policy and would like to be involved need to be included in its development. Parents and guardians who are interested in this issue should be included as well. If you don't have everyone's participation, you run the risk of not having their "buy-in." When this happens, the teachers, directors or supervisors, and family members involved may say that they understand and agree with the policy, but then may withhold their support and cooperation because they really don't.

It's true that some teachers or directors have developed holiday policies and made decisions about how to handle holidays that work well for them without consulting with families and co-workers. This solo approach is sometimes easier than organizing a group effort and working collaboratively with others. Also, if you work in a program where contact with families is limited, or in a part-year program where school starts after Labor Day, it can be hard to reach decisions collaboratively before the holidays are upon you. It's also true that educators have knowledge about child development and about working with children in a group setting that families may not have, and therefore there are some decisions that they may be better able to make.

However, this solo approach misses out on opportunities as well. One of the most valuable outcomes of bringing educators and families together to talk about goals for holidays is the thoughtful discussions that ensue (Katie Kissinger, 1992). These opportunities to share views and values are essential to a program using an inclusive, anti-bias approach. Holiday brainstorming meetings provide an opportunity for community building among educators and families. They provide avenues for people to get to know one another, hear each other's points of views, practice respectful listening, and learn about different values and practices. In addition, families deserve to be involved in curriculum decisions, particularly decisions about how holidays, which are so individual, personal, and important, will be handled. Given the opportunity, families often jump at the chance to have their voices heard and participate in the decision-making process. The teamwork among educators and families, and the shared ownership for the decisions that will emerge, will be very valuable.

Choose a Method

There are two general models of collaboration for developing your holiday policy:

The facilitator model

In the facilitator approach, one person takes the lead and is in charge of organizing the work and producing the final policy. In some programs this person is the director, a teacher, a parent or guardian, or a community member. The facilitator drafts sections of the policy and circulates them to other staff members and families for comments. Based on the feedback received, the facilitator then re-drafts and sends out the sections again. The process repeats until the facilitator has all of the information that she or he needs. The policy is then written. During this process, the facilitator may also call meetings and facilitate discussions, then draft sections of the policy based on that input.

This approach works well because the facilitator, who is ultimately in charge, keeps pushing forward the development of the policy. She or he keeps everyone on track, delegating the typing and copying of drafts, and supervising the distribution of drafts and the gathering of feedback. This approach is probably the most realistic and efficient for many early childhood programs given their organization and structure. The drawback to this approach is that it can be time-consuming for one person and doesn't involve other players as completely as the following approach.

The committee model

With the committee approach, a group of interested teachers, family members, administrators, board members, and other appropriate people meet on a regular basis to develop a policy. In some situations, the committee might put together some recommendations that will then go to some other authority, such as the director or board, for final approval.

The benefit to this approach is that it enables many different people in the school community to be involved in the policy in a major way. Programs that use this approach make a strong statement about their desire to include everyone. The drawback to this approach is that it can be unwieldy. It is difficult to find days and meeting times that work well for everyone, especially if you have a large committee. There also has to be a strong commitment and a lot of collaboration among committee members so that note-taking, typing, copying, distributing, and other tasks get done in a timely manner. With some committees, it is helpful to assign an organizer who takes care of or supervises these

Celebrate!

tasks. Some committees may need a point person to help keep them on track and move the process forward.

The prime distinction between the facilitator and the committee approaches is that with the facilitator, much of the information in the policy is birthed by the facilitator and then sent out to the school community for feedback. With the committee, all information is birthed within the committee at meetings. You may find that a single approach, an approach that combines the two, or some other model works best for your situation. The most important consideration is to make sure that no one who wants to be involved in the process is left out.

Set Your Own Ground Rules

Whatever collaborative approach you use to develop your holiday policy, everyone must understand clearly from the beginning what decisions can be influenced by those participating and what will be decided by a person or governing body in charge. It is very frustrating for people to think they are going to have an impact on policy, to put in effort and time, then find out that someone else really makes all the decisions. Be honest with other educators and family members about what decision-making power they truly have and what they don't. Let them know whether or not everyone will have an equal say. In most situations, there will be a director, teacher, board of directors, parent advisory committee, or someone else in charge who will make some final decisions.

If you are the person in charge, be sure that you know what your bottom lines are before asking for input. If there are certain things you absolutely want in your policy or definitely won't allow, say that at the beginning. For example, if you know that you will not allow violent or stereotypical costumes or decorations at Halloween, say so. If you cannot allow religious activities in your program, make sure everyone knows this before talking about Easter, Rosh Hashanah, or Ramadan.

Keep in mind, too, that it is likely that not everyone involved in the decision-making process will be able to agree on all aspects of your holiday policy. You or whoever is in charge should think about how to handle this situation if or when it arises.

Outline Your Policy

Develop a Holiday Policy

There are many components to a holiday policy. Each one answers a question about how holidays will be handled in your individual program. Below is a list of questions to consider as you decide what to include in your policy.

- **What are the goals and functions of holidays in the program?**

    What do you want to accomplish with holiday activities in the classroom?

    How do these goals relate to the children and families you work with? To your overall program goals and the anti-bias goals?

- **How important a place will holidays have in the program?**

    How much curriculum time will they take?

    How many holidays will you include each year?

    How much time will you spend on each holiday?

- **How will you make decisions about which holidays to include?**

    Who will make the decisions?

    How will families be involved?

    How will information be gathered from families?

    What role will teachers play? What role will the administration play?

- **In what ways will holidays be implemented in the curriculum?**

    Will you have parties? decorate? read books? play music?

    Will you discuss holidays at group-meeting times such as circle time?

    How will families be involved in holiday activities?

    How will teachers get the information they need to accurately portray a holiday?

    How will holiday activities reflect the overall classroom goals and specific goals for holidays?

    How will you make sure that all activities are developmentally appropriate?

    How will you make sure that holiday activities and discussions are connected to children's experiences?

    How will stereotypes in holidays be addressed?

Celebrate!

- How will you handle the religious aspects of holidays?

  Will holidays with a strong religious component be included?

  Will you talk about the religious component? In what way? Will teachers initiate the conversation? Or will it only emerge from the children?

- What is the plan for working with children and families who don't celebrate a holiday or holidays?

  How will you make sure that no child is excluded?

  What are the choices for these children?

- How will you evaluate the effectiveness of holiday activities?

  How will you get input from families about their perception of the success of holidays?

  How will teachers and directors or supervisors give input?

  What will you do with the information you receive?

On the next page is a sample holiday policy that addresses the components discussed above. Remember that this is just a sample and not a recipe to follow. Since your policy will reflect and meet the needs of the children and families you work with, your policy will probably look quite a bit different.

XYZ Child Care Center
Holiday Policy
April 1997

Definition of Holiday Activities

It is important to define holiday activities because the words "holiday" and "celebration" mean different things to different people. For purposes of this holiday policy and to define our holiday practices in the classroom, we define "holiday activities" in the following way.

Holiday activities at XYZ can be as simple as reading a book about a holiday and as elaborate and involved as having a party in the classroom with food, decorations, guests, and music. Activities often involve a group discussion about a holiday and how a family celebrates it, or the reading of a book about a holiday. Other times teachers set up open-ended, developmentally appropriate activities for children that relate to a holiday. We also have occasional parties to celebrate a holiday.

Goals and Functions of Holidays

1. To validate children's and families' holiday experiences and traditions at home.
2. To expose children to different ways of celebrating the same holiday.
3. To expose children to celebrations, traditions, and religions different from their own.
4. To foster respect for celebrations, traditions, and religions different from their own.
5. To provide fun and a break in the routine.
6. To mark time for children.
7. To build a sense of community, family, and togetherness.
8. To provide accurate information about holidays in a developmentally appropriate manner.
9. To encourage critical thinking about bias and unfairness.
10. To provide a stress-free environment.

(continued)

Role of Holidays in the Program

Since we plan curriculum on an emergent basis in a way that is reflective of children's needs and interests, the exact amount of time we spend on holidays will vary. We use children and families in the program as a "barometer" to help us decide how much we will do with holidays. We do have some guidelines, however, to make sure that holidays do not take over the entire curriculum. With regard to parties or actual celebrating, we will limit holiday parties to three or four per year. When we are "recognizing" a holiday (i.e. having a discussion or reading a book) or providing activities related to a holiday, we might include up to five holidays per month.

For example, on the Friday before Memorial Day, we will talk about the fact that the center is closed on the following Monday and explain why, in two or three sentences. When we are doing calendar every morning, we will talk with children about holidays that just occurred or that are imminently approaching. These recognitions of holidays, however, are no more than a two-minute discussion about what the holiday is called and what it is all about, unless children ask to know more. Similarly, when we provide activities, they will be open-ended and one of many choices so they are not the focus of the entire curriculum.

How Decisions Will Be Made About Which Holidays to Include

Individual decisions about which holidays will be included will be made every year and other times of the year when children and families leave or enter the program.

1. First, teachers and the director will use a variety of methods to determine what holidays are important to the children and families in the program. These will include a questionnaire, interviews, home visits, parent/guardian meetings, and daily communication.

2. Then teachers will make a list of any additional holidays they think are important to include. These include holidays they have incorporated in the past, social justice holidays, holidays that are celebrated by the staff, holidays that support overall classroom goals, and holidays that reinforce stereotypes or misinformation in order to provide opportunities for teachers to help children correct wrong impressions.

3. Next, teachers and the director will look at what holidays to include with which the children are unfamiliar. Before deciding to include any of these holidays, teachers will make sure they can introduce them in a relevant, respectful way that connects to children's own experiences.

(continued)

4. Teachers and the director will then look at the list they have generated so far and decide if anything else should be added to the list and if anything should be dropped from the list. Together they will make sure that all the chosen holidays meet at least one of the stated goals for holidays and that none of those holidays will offend or hurt any child or family.

How Holidays Will Be Implemented in the Curriculum

Below is a list of general guidelines we follow at XYZ as we implement holidays:

1. We are inclusive. We strive to validate everyone and exclude no one. We pay attention to the balance and the importance we put on certain holidays over others. No one holiday is portrayed as more important than any other.

2. We concentrate on reflecting a holiday in a way that is important and relevant to families at home.

3. We work to be culturally relevant in all of our activities. We portray holidays from the point of view of the person or group that celebrates those holidays. If teachers are not of the religious or cultural group that celebrates a certain holiday, we gather information from books and others who do celebrate the holiday.

4. We do our own research. Teachers learn what they can about a family's holiday that we are unfamiliar with before asking that family to supply information. This communicates respect and a genuine desire to obtain information.

5. We involve parents/guardians as much as possible in the implementation of holiday activities and celebrations. We also keep families informed of upcoming holiday activities and events.

6. We are careful to avoid stereotypes when presenting holiday information to children, putting up decorations, and implementing activities. We also are committed to addressing unfairness in holiday images and messages that children are experiencing outside of the classroom so they learn to recognize bias and hurtfulness.

7. We provide activities that are developmentally appropriate for the ages and stages of the children. Young children need concrete, hands-on activities with simple explanations. We are careful not to abandon all we know about good practices when it comes to holiday activities. We know that teacher-directed art and reproducible crafts that all look alike do not foster creativity or individual expression.

(continued)

©1997 *Celebrate! An Anti-Bias Guide to Enjoying Holidays in Early Childhood Programs.*
Redleaf Press, 10 Yorkton Court, St. Paul, MN 55117. 800-423-8309

8. We are sympathetic to the fact that holiday time can create hardships for some families due to financial constraints, family problems, etc. We are careful not to implement any activities that put financial pressure on families.

How Religious Aspects of Holidays Will Be Approached

While teachers won't teach the religious aspect of a holiday or teach one religion or religious holiday as the correct one, we will explain, in a developmentally appropriate way, what the historical meaning of that holiday is if children ask us directly for that information. Religious aspects will be explained matter-of-factly, with simple language. Families will be consulted for the actual language they use when talking about religious holidays to their children. Children will also be referred back to their families for more explanation and in-depth information about religious aspects of holidays. Aside from providing answers for children's direct questions about the religious aspects of holidays, teachers in general will avoid talking about religion without sacrificing the underlying meaning of a holiday. For example, we will explain that Christmas is a time for giving and sharing and Valentine's Day is a day of friendship and caring.

Plan for Working with Children and Families Who Don't Celebrate Holidays

We will not celebrate any individual holiday that excludes one or more children. If we have children in the program who do not celebrate any holidays, we will work with the families to come up with a plan for meeting their children's needs so they are not left out.

How We Will Evaluate the Effectiveness of Holiday Activities

We will be constantly reflective of holiday activities we have done in the past and how we might handle holidays in the future. Once a year, teachers, the director, and families will get together to talk about what is working, what isn't working, and to discuss future strategies.

©1997 *Celebrate! An Anti-Bias Guide to Enjoying Holidays in Early Childhood Programs.*
Redleaf Press, 10 Yorkton Court, St. Paul, MN 55117. 800-423-8309

Periodically Evaluate Your Policy

Like other components of an early childhood program, it is important to regularly evaluate the effectiveness of your holiday program. If possible, sit down with colleagues and families every twelve months or so and look at your holiday policy and overall approach to the holidays. Ask each other the following questions:

Develop a Holiday Policy

- How is the policy working? What are the overall strengths and weaknesses of our policy?

- Have we been handling holidays in ways that reflect our holiday goals and overall program goals?

- Is our method for deciding which holidays to include in the curriculum working?

- How effective are our methods for gathering information from families?

- Have families been involved in activities as much as we would like them to be and as much as they would like to be?

- How successful have we been at maintaining a fair and equitable balance among all the holidays? Are children or families getting a message that we consider some holidays more important or valuable than others?

- How well do we meet the needs of all the children and families in the program, both those who do and those who do not celebrate holidays?

- Are we satisfied with the way we have been handling the religious holidays?

- What effective strategies have we developed for dealing with stereotypes in holidays?

- Are there specific problems we have not been able to solve? What are they?

If families are not able to be a part of your discussion, consider sending out a simple questionnaire like the one on the next page to gather their input. Remember to translate questionnaires into the languages the families speak. Consider asking these questions in an informal interview if some families are more comfortable with that.

Sample Holiday Evaluation Questionnaire for Families

Dear Families,

It's time for us to take a look at how effective our holiday practices have been throughout the past year. Your input is critical to our evaluation process, and we would greatly appreciate it if you will answer the following questions and return the questionnaire to the office by next Monday.

1. Are you satisfied with our overall approach to holidays this past year?

    Please tell us why or why not:

2. What would you like us to add to our practices?

3. What would you like us to stop doing?

4. Did our activities and discussions this year adequately and accurately reflect your child and your family's rituals and celebrations? If so, how? If not, how can we improve?

5. Do you feel that there were enough opportunities for you to become involved in our activities? If not, how can we improve in this area?

6. What suggestions do you have for us in the next year?

Consider holding a parent or guardian meeting to discuss the findings of the questionnaire and to develop a plan for making improvements. All families may not be interested in attending. That's okay. Welcome those who are. The important thing is that all families are invited and encouraged to provide feedback in some way.

Be willing to alter your holiday policy to reflect the information you gather in the evaluation process. The holiday policy is meant to be flexible enough to grow as you do and to evolve to meet the changing needs of your families.

Develop a Holiday Policy

CHAPTER **5**

Determine Your Goals

Before you can really think about *what* to celebrate or *how* to implement holidays in programs for young children, it's necessary to think about *why* you want to do this. Like all well-planned curriculum, holiday activities need to have specific goals. Questions such as "What do I hope to accomplish?" and "What do I want children to get out of holiday activities?" will help you make conscious decisions about the use of holidays.

To develop your list, you'll need to work with colleagues and involve families and guardians. Read through the steps below first, then work together with others to arrive at agreed-upon goals. Keep in mind that collaboration can be challenging. You might want to review the section called "Acknowledge the Challenges of Collaboration" in chapter 3 for reminders and suggestions about working together. It might also be helpful to distribute and discuss the questionnaire on page 16, "What Filter Am I Using?" to get in touch with and understand one another's perspectives.

Consider Possible Goals

To get ideas for what your goals might be, read the four anti-bias goals that were developed by Louise Derman-Sparks, author with the Anti-Bias Task Force of *Anti-Bias Curriculum: Tools for Empowering Young Children* (NAEYC, 1989).

Celebrate!

Anti-Bias Curriculum Goals

1. To foster a positive self-identity within the context of a group identity.
2. To facilitate knowledgeable, empathic interactions with people who are different from oneself.
3. To foster critical thinking about bias.
4. To help children stand up for themselves and others in the face of bias.

The following curriculum goals were shared by educators who use an anti-bias approach in their program. Many of these goals are similar to the four anti-bias goals. You can decide which of these goals might fit in your program, along with additional goals that are not listed.

To promote connections among children, families, and staff

Holiday celebrations build and strengthen connections between home and school, and among children and/or teachers who share the same holidays. They also can promote a sense of community among children as they learn about one another's holidays and participate in activities together. The connection happens through the realizations that children have something in common. When Asma discovers that Hakeem also celebrates Ramadan, their friendship and esprit de corps is strengthened. Similarly, when Linda's mother comes in to make buñuelos for Cinco de Mayo, other children are invited to participate. Through this shared activity, a feeling of community emerges.

To learn about important events in the lives of all children and families in the program

Introducing holidays that are important to children and their families communicates respect and a commitment to be inclusive in classroom practices. Including these holiday activities in the curriculum provides an avenue for other children and adults to learn about these important events.

To support and validate the experiences of children, their families, and staff in the program

Holiday activities support children's experiences at home and in their communities, and thus strengthen positive feelings about and connections to their family and cultural group. Plainly, children get the message that what they do at home is valid and worth mention at school. This is especially valuable for children and families whose holidays are generally not reflected in the media, in store decorations, in children's books, and so on.

☀ TO REINFORCE CONNECTION TO CULTURAL ROOTS

Holiday rituals can reaffirm or deepen our connection to cultural roots, helping to teach or remind children of who they and their families are. These rituals can also give children a sense of security. They feel comfort in knowing that they will see some familiar sights, taste some familiar foods, and be together with people who are important to them. By including or talking about these same holiday rituals in the classroom, those reminders and feelings of comfort are also found at school.

☀ TO CELEBRATE BOTH SIMILARITIES AND DIFFERENCES IN THE CHILDREN'S LIVES

Holiday activities can show children in direct, meaningful ways that the same holidays can be celebrated differently, and that people often celebrate different holidays honoring events and beliefs unique to their ethnic groups. Activities can also point out to children the similar themes that run through many holidays, such as death, renewal, light and darkness, liberation, and harvest. Most important, holiday activities demonstrate that all holidays are important to the people who celebrate them and must be respected.

☀ TO STRETCH CHILDREN'S AWARENESS AND EMPATHY

Learning about holidays that are different from their own is one method for helping children move away from egocentric thinking and become aware of other people's ways of living. This can especially help children who celebrate the national holidays learn that what and how they celebrate isn't the one *right* or *only* way.

☀ TO TEACH CHILDREN CRITICAL THINKING ABOUT BIAS

Many holiday images and messages from television, radio, store decorations, books, magazines, and billboards unfortunately include gender, race, culture, class, and historical biases. Including these holidays in the curriculum provides opportunities to teach children how to examine what they see and hear for messages that are unfair or hurtful. Activities and discussions can also challenge children to consider the commercialization and mass marketing of certain holidays. These activities can lead children to understand that the inability to afford items doesn't make a family *bad* or *less than* other families.

☀ TO TEACH ACTIVISM

Empowering children to stand up for themselves and others is an important early childhood goal. By celebrating social justice holidays such as Passover, Martin Luther King, Jr.'s Birthday, and Mexican Independence Day, children learn about what real people struggled over in the past to create a better life for

Celebrate!

themselves and others. These celebrations can lead to discussions about people who are working for justice today.

To give children accurate information about specific holidays

Holiday activities can support what children learn at home and correct misconceptions they may have about other people's holidays. Activities can help children separate the commercial depiction from the actual meaning and history behind the holiday. Discussions can give children accurate information about the meaning behind the symbols, songs, smells, and other holiday artifacts and influences. This has particular relevance for children who are new to the United States and its holidays and do not understand the meaning of the symbols and rituals they see around them.

To mark time for children

Holiday celebrations can underscore certain times of the year by celebrating beginnings, endings, and other significant rhythms, such as seasonal changes. This has particular importance for twelve-month child care programs where there is seemingly no beginning and no end to the year.

To have fun

Holiday activities can be enjoyable. They add spice to daily life by providing a break in the usual routine. They can also bring feelings of anticipation, excitement, and magic into the classroom.

Consult Your Program Goals

To begin developing your own list, think about your overall goals for the children in your program. In some schools and centers, these may be predetermined by administrators, directors or supervisors, or a board of directors and written in program policies. In other cases, teachers can determine their own goals. There are many possibilities. You may have broad, overriding goals such as encouraging self-esteem and nurturing children's development in social, emotional, cognitive, physical, and creative ways. You may also have multicultural or anti-bias goals about helping children learn to value themselves and others, such as those previously explained in this chapter. And you may have more specific goals depending on the type of program you are in and what you think is most important for children.

Think About the Children and Families in Your Setting

Next, consider the children and families in your program. The goals you choose should be appropriate for their developmental levels, cultural backgrounds, and how similar or diverse they are as a group. For example, if you teach two year olds, your goals will be different than if you teach fives. (See chapter 8, "Remembering Developmentally Appropriate Practice," for detailed information about holidays and development.) If you teach children who are new to the country, your primary goals may be to foster connection between home and school, validate their home experiences, learn about important events in their lives, and offer information about the United States' holidays they see happening around them.

Reflect and Review

Think about and discuss your final list of goals. Keep in mind its importance, because it will steer the rest of the decisions you make about your holiday approach. At the same time, remember that your list can and should change to respond to changing circumstances.

CHAPTER **6**

Select Holidays

Once you are clear about your goals for holiday activities, you and others you are working with can start considering which of the many holidays you might celebrate will help you meet your goals. Of course, how you implement holiday activities will be essential to determining your overall success. The next section of the book, "Holidays in Your Classroom," gives you plenty of steps and strategies for implementation. But first, it's necessary to think about whether or not specific holidays merit inclusion in your curriculum at all.

You and your colleagues might want to begin this process by evaluating the holidays you have selected in the past. Take out the list of goals you developed in the last chapter. Then, under each goal, write down the holidays you included in your curriculum last year that relate to it. Are there any holidays that do not fit under any of the goals? It may be that you are including a holiday just because you enjoy it personally and want to celebrate it, not because it is important and meaningful for your children. Are there any holidays that fit under only one goal (such as "to have fun"), and don't seem as important to include given your other goals? Are there any holidays on the list that meet one or more of your goals, but that may be hurtful or offensive to any child or family?

After you've reviewed you current practices—or if you didn't celebrate any holidays last year or you just prefer to start fresh—you can begin to work together to develop a list of holidays to celebrate now.

Celebrate!

Gather Information From Families

If you look back at the end of chapter 2 and at your goals list, you'll likely see a strong emphasis on learning about and reflecting children's home experiences. Clearly, in order to meet these goals, you will need to gather considerable information from children's parents and guardians. Your primary purpose will be to learn all you can about what holidays families celebrate and how they celebrate them so you can be inclusive and reflect families' home practices. It will also be helpful to learn the religious backgrounds and beliefs of each family, since religion plays such a large role in holidays. In addition, some families may object to their child being exposed to certain holidays, and some families don't celebrate any holidays at all. This is also important information to get. (Chapter 13 offers ideas and strategies for meeting these families' needs.)

Naturally you will need to be sensitive and respectful to the families you speak with. To do that, your conversations about holidays must take place in the context of solid relationships between you and families. Turn back to "Evaluate Your Home/School Relationships" in chapter 3, and decide whether you are ready to proceed with the next step in the process.

Select Your Methods

When you are ready, you can begin the process of communicating with families about their holiday practices at home. There are many good methods to use. Here are examples to choose from or to use in combination.

Questionnaires

Send out a questionnaire asking families what special days they celebrate at home and how they celebrate them. The more precise you are about the information you wish to have, the better responses you will get. For example, the sample questionnaire on the next page asks for specific information such as the importance of holidays to families, how families want their holidays to be reflected in the classroom, and other pertinent questions. Be sure to include on your questionnaire an explanation of why this information is needed. Also, remember to translate questionnaires (and all other communication) into the languages that families use.

Sample Family Questionnaire About Holidays

Dear Families,

Your answers to the following questions will help us greatly in our efforts to develop an inclusive, sensitive approach to holiday celebrations and to planning activities appropriate for your children's ages and developmental levels. Thank you for taking the time to fill this out. Please return it to the office by 8/1.

1. On a scale of 1–10, how important are holidays to your family? (One is unimportant and ten is essential.)

2. What special days do you celebrate in your family? How do you celebrate them?

3. How would you like the program to support or reflect your celebrations? Or, if your family does not celebrate any holidays, how would you prefer us to work with you and your child if/when we have holiday activities in our program?

4. What would you like your child to gain from holiday activities while in our program?

5. What concerns do you have about holiday activities?

6. How do you feel about your child learning about or participating in holiday activities that are not part of your family's tradition? Are there any holidays you would object to?

7. Religion plays an important role in many holidays. While considering these next questions, please keep in mind that teachers would not teach any religious perspective as the "right" religion, rather we would always say "Some people believe . . ." or "At Sally's house, they believe . . ."

   7a. What religious holidays, if any, do you celebrate in your home?

   7b. How do you feel about your child experiencing in our program the religious aspects of holidays you celebrate in your family?

   7c. How do you feel about your child being exposed to religious aspects of a holiday that your family may not believe in?

8. How would you like to participate in holiday activities in the classroom?

©1997 *Celebrate! An Anti-Bias Guide to Enjoying Holidays in Early Childhood Programs.*
Redleaf Press, 10 Yorkton Court, St. Paul, MN 55117. 800-423-8309

Celebrate!

Family meetings

Hold a meeting to explain to parents and guardians why you want to learn about family holidays. Allow time and answer any questions to gain their trust about how you will use the information families give. Consider combining this approach with distributing questionnaires. One strategy to ensure participation is to hand out the questionnaires at the meeting and encourage parents or guardians to fill them out before they leave. You can also interview family members individually who are not comfortable using a written questionnaire.

If, while you are gathering information, a discussion arises about issues such as what holidays to include or what parents and guardians would like to see happen in your approach to holidays, be prepared for strong reactions and emotions. You may need to support people who express opinions that are counter to what most of the group feels and wants. Assure everyone that you and/or others who are making decisions will take everyone's feelings and needs into account as much as possible and will strive to meet everyone's individual needs. Offer to meet individually with families to discuss concerns.

Home visits

If you do home visits, consider asking for holiday information then. If you have already conducted all your home visits for this year, keep this strategy in mind when planning for the next year.

Informal conversations

Drop-off and pick-up times in schools or child care settings can be a good time to gather additional information. Telephone calls to parents or guardians at pre-determined, agreed-upon times is another strategy. Phone conversations may work very well for some families, especially if they do not have the time to fill out a questionnaire or just feel more comfortable talking rather than writing out their responses.

Community participation

Teachers can learn a lot about what and how families celebrate simply by being present in their communities. If you don't live in the same neighborhoods as your families, make an effort to visit them both during holiday time and at other times of the year. For example, shop in the grocery store, walk down the street, play in the park, and attend a holiday festival or other cultural event that is open to everyone. You will learn a lot about the families' daily lives as well as their holidays if you spend time in their communities. Families will trust and respect you more if they see you regularly in their communities.

Support Reluctant Families

Select Holidays

Families whose holiday celebrations are very different from what they perceive others' to be may be particularly concerned about how you will use the information you gather. Sometimes these families are reluctant to share information because they are concerned that their child will seem too different if her or his unique holiday rituals or activities are included in the program. Other families may be willing to share information, but will ask that you not plan activities around their special day. There are a myriad of reasons for families to feel this way. Some families may prefer that special holiday activities not happen at school so that their child will look forward to the festivities at home. Others may feel it is inappropriate to do certain holiday activities with children outside their own community of people.

It is necessary for these and all families to trust that the private information shared with you will be used respectfully and sensitively. Ongoing dialogue with families about the purpose for the information and how it will be used will help to ease apprehension. But if parents or guardians would simply rather not share information, this decision must be respected and supported.

Points to Remember

As you gather information from families, keep these points in mind.

- Asking about holidays is only one piece of the overall task of respectfully learning about each family's culture. Finding out about their day-to-day lives is equally important.

- If you think families celebrate holidays that are different from yours, learning a little about the holidays before asking for information will go a long way in building trust and showing that your interest is sincere.

- Don't assume that everyone from an ethnic group celebrates the same holiday or celebrates a shared holiday in the same way. Similarly, be aware that some families who are multiracial may not celebrate all the holidays related to their diverse cultural or ethnic backgrounds. Ask each individual family to share information so no assumptions are made.

- Keep in mind that although at first glance a program may seem to be fairly homogenous (i.e. all European Americans or all Spanish speakers), a deeper look will uncover much diversity. Differences in religion, socioeconomic class, and family styles and practices may be abundant. These differences are important to recognize, learn about, and celebrate.

Celebrate!

Review Your Information About Families

When you finish gathering information, you can develop your draft list of holidays. Begin by writing down all the holidays that families celebrate at home, that are important to them, and that they consent to have you celebrate in your classroom.

You may discover that including all of the special days listed would require having more holiday activities than you want in your curriculum. This is particularly likely if families in your program come from many different cultures or religions. You don't have to include all of every family's holidays, but you should make sure that at least one or two of each family's holidays are recognized. One strategy is to look for a few holidays that are important to many different families and make sure to include those. Remember to recognize the one or two most important days for each remaining family as well.

Caution

When choosing holidays, some teachers feel that it is more important to include those that are not validated and reflected in the larger society. Since some holidays, especially Christmas, are so pervasive in our society, it may seem unnecessary to include them in the curriculum. However, young children don't understand this logic. If Christmas is a holiday that is important to them and their family, they deserve to have it reflected in the program just as much as other holidays. The "leaving out" approach might also make some family members feel angry or hurt that your "sensitive, inclusive" approach to holidays excludes them.

Also remember that while it's okay not to include *all* of everyone's holidays, it is very important to look for a variety of ways, besides holidays, to represent families' cultures. For ideas, look for the box in chapter 9, "Culture Throughout Your Curriculum."

Find Out About Program Requirements

Some early childhood programs may have policies or regulations in place that will influence which holidays you can celebrate in your classroom. For example, a religious-based program such as those associated with a church, temple, or mosque, may require certain religious holidays each year. A publicly-funded program may restrict religious celebrations but require that some national holidays be recognized. Find out if any rules such as these will effect your decisions and add these days to your list.

There may also be holidays expected, though not officially required, by the agency you are in. These expectations may differ, depending if your program is located in an elementary school or high school or on a college campus, for example. In some instances, students or faculty at these schools organize events to celebrate holidays, such as Cinco de Mayo or Halloween. In those cases, it may be important for you to include those holidays in some way.

Add Your Own Choices

Next, add to your list holidays that, as an educator, you feel offer valuable experiences for young children or that are important for the community in which you work. Here are a few categories to consider.

Holidays that support classroom goals

Selected holidays can highlight the overall goals you and your children work toward all year and are relevant for every child in your program. For example, introducing activities for Mohandas Ghandi's Birthday (October 2) or Peace Day (May 18) can support classroom goals of promoting peace and nonviolence. Similarly, Susan B. Anthony's Birthday on February 15 provides an opportunity to highlight strong girls and women and changing things that aren't fair, two other possible program goals.

Holidays that commemorate social justice

Holidays that commemorate struggles for justice, peace, and freedom provide examples for children of people who worked hard to correct unfair situations. Celebrating these holidays can lead to discussions about what children can do when things are unfair in their lives and about adult leaders who are working for justice today. The Fourth of July, which celebrates the adoption of the Declaration of Independence, and Martin Luther King, Jr.'s Birthday, which celebrates one important man in the struggle for civil rights, are two examples of these holidays.

Holidays to broaden children's perspectives

If one of your goals for holidays is to stretch children's awareness, empathy, and understanding of similarities and differences, but the children in your program celebrate the same holidays in similar ways, you might consider introducing holidays that no one in the classroom celebrates. If your children are at least three years old, introducing these holidays can help them understand that people celebrate different holidays in various ways and that all of them are valid. On the other hand, introducing unfamiliar cultural holidays easily leads to a "tourist" approach. When this happens, your goals of teaching empathy and understanding can actually be undermined. Deciding whether or not to introduce these holidays requires a lot of thought. See chapter 10, "Introducing Unfamiliar Holidays," for information and ideas.

Celebrate!

Caution

Even if your children all celebrate the same holidays, you can teach about similarities and differences by focusing on the wide variations in the ways people celebrate. Don't feel like you must expose your children to unfamiliar cultural holidays to accomplish this goal. In fact, it may be preferable not to.

Holidays that provide critical thinking opportunities

Some holidays children are exposed to every year contain stereotypes or perpetuate misinformation about a historical event or group of people. Depending on the ages of the children in your classroom, you might include some of these holidays as a strategy for directly addressing the stereotypes children are learning about and for promoting critical thinking. For example, Thanksgiving can be one of the times you discuss stereotypes about Native Americans, and at Halloween you can talk about stereotypes of older women and the color black. Many holidays have also become highly commercialized in our society. Discussing that issue with children around Christmas, Halloween, Thanksgiving, Valentine's Day, or Easter, for example, is another way to help children become critical thinkers and help them resist the impact of consumerism. Chapter 11, "Addressing Stereotypes and Commercialism," offers a discussion of these issues and strategies for addressing them.

Classroom culture holidays

You might have invented holidays that you celebrate every year and that have become a part of your classroom culture. These should also be on your list. They may not be special to any other group of children in any other program, but they have particular meaning and relevance for your group. And they are a wonderful way to build connections and a sense of community among children and teachers in your room. Just a few of the many possible examples of invented holidays used in classrooms are Backwards Day, where regular classroom practices and routines are reversed; Tea Party celebrations, when children bring in their favorite dolls or teddy bears for a tea party; or Wheel Day, when children and adults bring to school a bike, skateboard, wagon, roller skates, or other wheeled toy to ride during outside time. If your program does special birthday celebrations for children or end-of-the-year events such as graduation ceremonies, these can be considered invented holidays as well.

Community holidays

Some programs include holiday celebrations that are of special local importance. For example, in Joseph, Oregon, a small town north of Portland, many schools and child care programs celebrate Chief Joseph Day since their town is named after this important peace activist. In other communities there may be a clambake, a tulip festival, or many other possible days to celebrate.

Current events

Important happenings that children will be exposed to during the year may influence your holiday decisions. The 1992 Quincentennial Celebration of Columbus' "discovery" was one example. Similarly, if the country is in the midst of a war, then Veterans Day may be a holiday to include on your list.

Evaluate Your List

At this point you'll need to go back and assess how you are doing in your selection process. Keep in mind that the holidays in your classroom will probably differ from those in the classroom next door or down the hall. This is a good sign! It means that you are including holidays that meet the specific needs of the children and families in your classroom.

The holiday goals you decided on in the previous chapter are your overriding guideline when choosing holidays now. Take time to go over each holiday on your current list and be clear about how it relates to your selected goals. Make sure that you haven't kept any holidays on your list just because you've always done them. When you are done, consider asking families for their responses to your final list. Verify that their important days are represented, and find out if they are uncomfortable with any of the holidays included.

You may find that you now have too many holidays and need to pare down your list. Whether or not that is true, the following strategies can help you in your evaluation.

Set a standard

It might be helpful to decide on a number of goals that a holiday must meet in order to be included in your program. This is especially useful if you are trying to limit the number of holidays on your list. Two or three goals are a good baseline.

Prioritize goals according to your group

Try to identify which goals are the most important for the group of children and families you work with. For example, if your children are all European American, the main goals may focus on connections, becoming aware of the diversity in the ways that different European American families celebrate, exploring holidays that are celebrated in the community but not in the program, and helping children realize that theirs isn't the only or right way to celebrate. If your children are all children of color and they celebrate some holidays that

Celebrate!

aren't represented outside of their homes, one of the most important goals might be validation of what the children and families celebrate, in order to nurture positive self-esteem and group identities. Creating opportunities for connections would also be an important goal. With a very diverse group with both children of color and European American children, the main goals might focus on validation of each child and expanding on the many similarities and differences among them.

Consider religion

Be aware of the strong religious components that are part of many holidays. If teaching about religion is not a goal for you or is not appropriate to your setting (as it might be in a religious-based program), decide whether you will be able to include the holiday while avoiding this aspect (see chapter 12 for information and strategies).

Remember your bottom line

No matter how many goals a holiday may meet, if a specific holiday activity hurts any one child or family in any way, or teaches hurtful information, consider carefully whether you will continue to include this activity in the curriculum. For example, children may enjoy wearing Indian headdresses and acting out the first Thanksgiving, but that practice can severely hurt Native American children in the classroom and the other children's growing sense of who Native American people are. Similarly, celebrating Cinco de Mayo may seem like a good way to celebrate similarities and differences, but if no one in the classroom or community celebrates it, and it is the only activity about Mexican Americans that you celebrate, then it becomes a "tourist" activity.

CHAPTER **7**

Evaluate Holiday Activities

Once you have assessed your situation, begun a holiday policy, and decided about your goals for holiday activities and the holidays you will include, you will be ready to begin implementing your new approach in the classroom. The next section of this book will offer guidance for the many questions and issues you might face.

But as you implement your activities, it's important to remember the last step in the process of change: evaluating. When you evaluate your activities on a regular basis, you help to ensure that they will continue to meet the needs of the children and accomplish what you intend them to. By continually evaluating and re-evaluating practices, you give yourself opportunities to improve. Eventually you will develop practices that accomplish your goals and meet the changing needs of children and families. Follow these steps to guide you in your efforts.

Meet to Review Your Activities

Set aside time shortly after each holiday passes to sit down with other staff members, and parents and guardians if possible, to talk about what worked and what didn't in your activities. Ask the following questions:

- How do we feel about including this holiday in the curriculum? Did we choose to include it for good reasons? How were children and families involved in making the decision?

- How well did the holiday activities we implemented and the discussions we had with children accomplish what we wanted them to?

- What messages did we give children through this holiday?

- How did families respond to the way we handled this holiday? What feedback, if any, did we get from them?

- Are we satisfied with the amount of knowledge we had about this holiday? Did we have adequate materials?

- Did we portray this holiday in relevant ways for the children and families in the program who celebrate it? How were they involved in planning for and/or implementing the holiday activities?

If the holiday you are reviewing was one that neither you nor the children in the program celebrate, ask the following additional questions:

- If I were a member of the group that celebrates this holiday, how would I feel about this representation of me and my holiday?

- If this were the first time I had heard about this holiday, what is one thing I would gain from this experience?

- Did we implement curriculum around this holiday within the context of connections that we and the children have made with people who celebrate it as part of their culture or religion?

- How authentically were the holiday and the people represented? Were there times that we accidentally transmitted misinformation?

- Did we successfully avoid making this holiday seem exotic? Did the activities connect to other experiences so children could relate to it?

Plan for Improvement

Agree together on a plan for improving your approach. Try using the questions on the next page, or another tool that meets your needs. Remember that the first time you try out an activity, you may not be entirely satisfied with it. With more experience, information, feedback, and planning, your practices will get better. Keep at it!

Holiday Practices Improvement Plan

Things we did really well:

Things we would like to improve:

Ideas for next time:

HOLIDAYS IN YOUR CLASSROOM

CHAPTER 8

Remembering Developmentally Appropriate Practice

Now comes the fun part. So far in this book you've looked at holiday curriculum in new ways and thought about or perhaps begun the process of changing your approach. Now it's time to step into the classroom and talk about how to create holiday activities that are relevant and enjoyable for everyone.

The main ingredient for successful holiday activities is the same as it is for all good early childhood curriculum. It involves understanding developmentally appropriate practice and planning engaging activities that have meaning to children and meet their developmental needs. Yet for some reason, when it comes to holidays, it's all too common to lose sight of all we know about early childhood curriculum planning. For example, early childhood teachers know that a three year old's concept of time is very limited and generally tied to familiar, real events, such as the next time she wakes up in the morning or what comes next on the daily schedule. However, it is not uncommon for teachers of three year olds to introduce units about the first story of Thanksgiving, an event that happened hundreds of years ago. Similarly, many teachers work hard all year

long to provide art activities that are process-oriented. However, it is common for those same teachers to encourage children to paint a red, heart-shaped cutout at Valentine's Day, to glue cotton balls on a bunny shape at Easter, or to make hand prints on tie shapes for a Father's Day present.

At this point, consider taking some time to review the abundance of material about the cognitive stages of young children that is available to you as an early childhood educator. Janice Hale, Lillian Katz, Jawanza Kunjufu, Wade Nobles, Carol Brunson Phillips, Jean Piaget, Lev Vygotsky, and Amos Wilson have contributed greatly to our understanding of how young children develop and learn. NAEYC's publication *Developmentally Appropriate Practices-Revised* is another important resource. Reflect on the information you already have or refer to these authors for new information to guide you. They will tell you that:

- ▶ young children can be egocentric and believe that their thoughts and experiences are universal.

- ▶ very young children learn through their actions and need concrete, hands-on experiences.

- ▶ young children have a variety of basic needs, concerns and fears.

Of course all children develop at different rates and learn concepts at different times, but there are also stages that most children go through. The chart and the information below provide a general, year-by-year profile of how children understand and respond to holidays from ages two to five. Use this information to guide you in planning age-appropriate activities.

Holiday Ages and Stages

Two year olds:

- enjoy being with their families on holidays
- can catch excitement from adults, but don't understand what holidays are
- may be overstimulated or upset by too much change in routine

Three year olds:

- view holiday celebrations in terms of their own family experiences
- are egocentric and think that everyone celebrates what they do and in the same way
- need to see their family's special holidays reflected in their school environment, especially if the holidays are not usually visible in our society

- learn from holiday activities that are concrete, accurate, and connected to their own experiences
- understand and respond to the feelings holidays bring, rather than to the reasons people celebrate them
- may not remember anything about a particular family celebration from last year

Four year olds:

- continue to view holidays primarily in terms of their own family experiences
- continue to need to see their family's special holidays reflected in their school environment
- may remember a celebration from last year and look forward to it
- begin to realize that some people celebrate holidays other than their own, and celebrate in different ways
- can talk about similarities and differences among holidays that connect to their own experiences
- understand simple (and accurate) information about the meanings of holidays

Five year olds:

- enjoy celebrating holidays with friends as well as with families
- continue to need to see their family's special holidays reflected in their school environment
- enjoy preparing for celebrations by making special foods, decorating, etc.
- want celebrations to be consistent "like last year"
- understand that people celebrate different holidays and enjoy learning about them
- begin understanding the historical or social reasons why a holiday is celebrated

Work With Children

Following are activity ideas for children in different age groups.

Working with twos

It may not be appropriate to talk directly about holidays with children younger than two. For two-year-old children the focus might be on a decoration they can look at and touch, or a food item they can taste and smell, or a familiar holiday music tape to listen to. If these ideas sound appropriate for your children, invite families to bring in something from home that their child might recognize and connect with a holiday. It could be a few evergreen branches, cookies

Celebrate!

(or a recipe to make cookies that you could do with the children), pomander balls (oranges with cloves in them), a diva (lamp for Diwali), a kinara (candle-holder for Kwanzaa), or a music tape. Avoid too much explanation of the holiday with this age group. Limit discussions to information such as "Molly brought evergreen branches from the Christmas tree at her house to share with us. I'll put them on the table here so you can touch and smell them," or "This is the kinara that Michael and his family light during Kwanzaa. Maybe we'll light it at nap time and watch the candles glow," or simply "This is music from Maya's house."

With twos and some older children, it can be helpful to wait to have relevant discussions until after a holiday, when children's experiences with their families are fresh in their minds and stories about what they did at home will naturally emerge.

Working with threes

Threes are ready for simple activities that reflect what their families do at home. They are still very sensory oriented and need opportunities to taste, smell, touch, and listen to materials in order for them to be meaningful and appropriate. Cooking and baking are favorite activities that appeal to most threes. Consider inviting a family member to share a recipe or, better yet, lead the children in a cooking activity! Many children of this age also love to sing. Holiday-related songs that children or families share may be an appropriate circle time activity. (See chapter 12 for thoughts about religious songs.) Discussions about holidays at this age must be kept to a minimum. You'll probably find a few children who want to talk a lot about a holidays while others are bored and ready for a new activity. Their attention spans and ability to remember what happened last year is limited at this age. Threes love books and may be quite interested in a holiday-related book, especially one they brought from home.

Working with fours

Fours are ready for conversations about holidays, especially their own! Many of them will remember family celebrations from last year and will likely be involved in putting up decorations and making other preparations for this year's upcoming holidays at home. They are also ready to begin talking about the different holidays people celebrate. Try making a graph with them that pictorially shows how many children in the room celebrate Christmas, Santa Lucia, Hanukkah, Kwanzaa, Solstice, or new year's days during the winter months. In the spring, you might graph Passover, Easter, Now-Ruz, and St. Patrick's Day. In the fall, Dia de Los Muertos, Yom Kippur, Rosh Hashanah, Thanksgiving, and Halloween are just a few of the appropriate days to graph. Books are a wonderful way to represent and introduce holidays at this age. Fours love to be read to and to "read" themselves. Songs are a favorite too. Invite families to share favorites from home or from their childhoods.

Art activities need to be open-ended and focus on process over product. Provide materials so children in this age group who want to can make gifts (anything they choose), wrap presents in hand-made wrapping paper, or create cards or decorations. Fours also enjoy socio-dramatic play and will role-play holiday events and happenings when given the opportunity. Consider putting holiday-related props in the house area. Some examples are empty valentine candy boxes, miniature flags from a variety of countries, gourds, pumpkins, a cornucopia, fancy dress-up clothes, cookie and cake mix boxes, candleholders (kinara, menorah, diva, advent wreath), a mini Christmas tree, evergreen branches, dreidels, and pictures of individuals and families celebrating.

Working with fives

Fives like to plan and can usually handle longer-term projects. If you choose to have an involved holiday-related activity, such as planning a party or other event, fives often enjoy the brainstorming, orchestrating, and problem solving that goes with it. Consider posing the idea to them at a circle time or at the lunch table, and if there is interest, make a list of all the things you will need for the party or other event. Talk about what needs to happen and assign working groups where, for example, group one is responsible for refreshments, group two's job is to make invitations, group three will be responsible for decorations, and so on. With a project like this, there are opportunities to work on small motor skills (making invitations), math (counting how many places to set), science (baking), large motor skills (putting up decorations), and social development (working together, problem solving, assigning roles).

Even with this age, however, limit the planning and festivities to only a few days. Ask families to help by coming in and working with one of the groups or by donating or lending materials from home. Fives love to talk about the way they do things at home and enjoy bringing in a special decoration or book to share with the group. Fives also like to talk about the fact that different people celebrate different holidays and the many ways that people celebrate the same holiday. Their interests open many opportunities for expansion of the concept of similarities and differences.

Keep Holiday Activities in Check

Too many holidays coming too often and bombarding children with food, decorations, and music is a problem in many programs. These activities are exciting but can be too exciting, overstimulating young children and neglecting their need for familiar, predictable routines. The following are some basic strategies

for corralling holiday activities so they are meaningful and fun, yet don't take over the curriculum.

Talk about holidays rather than celebrating

Not every holiday activity has to mean a party. Sometimes it is more appropriate to hold discussions or read books about a holiday, or to have family members talk about how they celebrate at home. Here's an example.

In one child care program, many families celebrate Chinese New Year. In honor of this holiday, Lisa's family brought in a Chinese calendar, Nicholas brought in a book about Chinese New Year, Wesley brought in some Lei See (red envelopes with lucky money inside, traditionally given out on Chinese New Year), and a couple of families brought in different paper lions similar to the ones they would see at the Lion Dance in Chinatown that weekend. At circle time, the teacher talked a little about the holiday these families would be celebrating. The class shared the paper lion Mei-Ling's family brought and Mei-Ling described how she was afraid of the huge lion head that the dancers carried during last year's parade, but how she wouldn't be this year. Then the teacher read the book about Chinese New Year. The discussion concluded with Wesley distributing the Lei See to the children. No additional activities were planned, although the children did on occasion ask to have the children's book read to them again.

This approach works especially well when there is a holiday that requires attention but is not developmentally appropriate to delve into. For example, children who attend a child care program housed in a public school may notice pictures of past United States presidents on bulletin boards and may ask about these men. It is appropriate and necessary for you to answer questions and offer a simple explanation of what President's Day is about. However, because these men who lived long ago don't have particular relevance in their own lives, young children will not understand much about them. Therefore it's not useful to explain the holiday in great detail or plan activities around this day.

FIT HOLIDAYS INTO YOUR REGULAR ROUTINES

Introduce activities that allow you to adhere to your routines as much as possible. Holiday activities that last for more than a day or two or that include a lot of sugary snacks, large parties where families visit and stay through lunch and nap time, or coaching children to memorize songs for a presentation can all be too much for young children. Set up holiday art or decorating activities during your regular free choice or activity time. Have families visit for a short meal at the usual lunch time so children still have time to nap. Learn songs together as you generally would and invite families to participate in a sing-along instead of a pressured performance. Throughout your holiday activities, observe children closely to make sure they do not become overstimulated by people, activities, or food.

Avoid centering classroom themes around a holiday

It's best not to make any holiday the entire focus of your curriculum for an extended time. In some programs, for example, teachers turn December into one giant holiday activity. This approach not only over-stimulates children but it also leaves out a lot of other wonderful activities and curriculum themes that are meaningful to and reflective of the children. Furthermore, children who don't celebrate that particular holiday feel left out for a very long time.

Remembering
Developmentally
Appropriate Practice

Steer away from activities that scare children

It is common for young children to be frightened by masks and people dressed up in costumes for Halloween. This is partly due to the difficulty young children have distinguishing between reality and fantasy. Similarly, children might be afraid of the lion's head carried by dancers in the Lion Dance performed at Chinese New Year, or of a "real" Santa Claus. Look for ways to avoid the scary aspects of these rituals and still create opportunities for fun. For example, instead of inviting children to come to preschool or child care wearing their costumes and masks, provide a wide variety of dress-up clothing and materials for making masks at school. Introduce a smaller model of the lion carried in Chinese New Year dances instead of a full-sized version.

Offer activities that calm children and focus on process

Holiday-related projects that allow for individual process and creativity provide a nice balance for more hectic activities and large social gatherings. Here are a few examples of activities to provide.

▶ Supply materials for children to sponge-paint or spatter-paint on newsprint or construction paper, to make homemade wrapping paper that can be used for holiday gift-giving or any occasion.

▶ Create a card-making center for any holiday, which includes materials such as card stock, scrap paper, doilies, metallic paper, markers, stickers, glitter, glue, scissors, staplers, old holiday cards, used wrapping paper, ribbon, rubber stamps and pads, and other materials. Children can make cards to give away or just experiment with the materials.

▶ Invite children to work with clay to create a holder for a candle. Provide clay, sequins, buttons, and glitter. Use clay that dries well; then children can paint them a day or two later. This fits well with holidays that share the common theme of light, as many December holidays do.

▶ Water play, digging in sand, and making and molding playdough are activities that are always calming and appropriate for holidays. To make them more festive, try adding holiday-related colors to sand or water in

the sensory table or spices to playdough. These sensory experiences may trigger holiday thoughts or memories for some children.

Offer a variety of open-ended materials

For art or craft projects, combine holiday and non-holiday possibilities that allow children to create anything they choose. For example, if you are setting out tissue paper and pipe cleaners so children can make paper flowers for Cinco de Mayo, include additional types of paper, fabric scraps, and glue for collages. Or you could supply plastic bottles and liquid starch along with the tissue paper so children have the option to make "stained-glass" vases.

Provide a selection of holiday-related and other activities

To meet children's developmental needs, you'll want to have activities available every day that address all areas of development, including language, math, science, small motor skills, creative, cognitive, and social development. But instead of trying to fit all of these into a holiday theme, consider making one or two of the activities holiday-related. The remaining ones can focus on other topics that are relevant and interesting to children at the time, such as changing seasons, new babies, spaceships, or growing things.

Choose Appropriate Themes

As early childhood educators we know how to use the best of an activity or material and leave the rest. We read books and leave out certain inappropriate passages, and we alter songs so that the little white duck is sometimes a girl and sometimes a boy. Instead of throwing away puzzles that show Asian children with slits for eyes, we use a permanent marker to make the eyes a bit more almond-shaped.

The same can be done with holiday activities. You can pick and choose aspects of a holiday to focus on without losing the essence or meaning of the holiday. This can be useful in making activities developmentally appropriate, and for other reasons such as including all children, emphasizing the most meaningful parts of holidays, and avoiding commercialism and materialism.

Sometimes a new angle on a holiday is all that's needed to make it more suitable for an early childhood curriculum. Here are ideas for creative approaches to a few holidays that can present problems.

Mother's and Father's Day

Mother's Day and Father's Day are very special for some families. Children naturally enjoy making things for their parents and others, and making gifts for Mother's or Father's Day is a natural extension of this. However, given the diversity in the kinds of families in our society, traditional ways of celebrating these days may no longer work. Encouraging children to make gifts for mothers on Mother's Day is not appropriate and can be very hurtful for a child whose only parent is her or his father. Similarly, putting out materials for children to make Father's Day gifts doesn't work for a child who has two moms and no dad. You can avoid putting a child or family in an uncomfortable situation by celebrating a "Family Day" instead. This allows children from any family configuration to be included. Make materials available so children who want to can make gifts or cards for anyone in their family: mother, father, grandparent, uncle, brother, godmother, stepparent, foster parent, big sister or brother, and so on.

Remembering Developmentally Appropriate Practice

Valentine's Day

Valentine's Day is a holiday that has been very influenced by commercial interests. This is unfortunate because there are some wonderful themes in this holiday that are meaningful to young children: friendship and caring. One program in southern California has modified Valentine's Day, calling it Appreciation Day, instead, and incorporating the meaningful themes while avoiding the commercial influence (ReGena Booze, 1988). Prior to Appreciation Day, the children make a list of everyone in the school community that helps to make their days easier. The list includes people like the secretary, the director, the cleaning crew, the handy person, the gardeners, the person who cooks the meals, and others. The teachers talk to the children about how lucky they are to have these special people helping to take care of them and helping to make sure that everything that needs to get done at school does. A day or so before Appreciation Day (which happens on or around February 14), the children make and deliver invitations, inviting all of these people to come to their classroom for muffins, juice, and other treats. A group of children and adults bake muffins for the party and put them out on the table just in time for the guests to arrive.

Thanksgiving

Thanksgiving is a difficult holiday to present to children for several reasons. First, it recognizes an event that happened hundreds of years ago, too long ago for young children to grasp. Second, it relays, in a one-sided manner, a part of history that has more than one side. Third, it often reinforces misinformation and negative stereotypes about Native Americans. One way to make this holiday meaningful for young children and avoid its inappropriate aspects is to focus on the more general concepts of harvest and thankfulness, rather than the historical aspects. These are two themes that children know about and can relate to.

Teachers can introduce activities about foods and where they come from. Discussions can follow about which foods are the children's favorites and all

the things they are most thankful for. There are many opportunities for science, math, and creative and language arts activities. Here are some examples for extending the themes of harvest and thankfulness.

- ▶ Take a field trip to a nearby grocery store, farm, or vegetable stand. Buy vegetables to take back to the classroom, and make soup.

- ▶ Cut open a pumpkin, squash, and gourd, and separate the seeds from the flesh. Invite children to sort and count the seeds. Make a graph and see which had the most seeds. Try baking the seeds and having a taste test. Set aside seeds to be planted in the spring in the classroom's garden.

- ▶ Make homemade pumpkin pie or sweet potato pie.

- ▶ Wash and bake potatoes or make mashed potatoes.

- ▶ Make popcorn.

- ▶ Invite children from another classroom to come over one day at lunch time for a harvest party.

- ▶ At circle time hang up a big piece of paper that says "Things we are thankful for" and invite children to add to the list (Regena Booze, 1988).

- ▶ Have book-making materials available so children can write stories about foods and other things they are thankful for.

The overriding theme here is that people in all cultures and countries celebrate and are thankful for the food they have to eat. They are also thankful for having family, friends, and a safe place to sleep.

Martin Luther King, Jr.'s Birthday

This is an important holiday because it highlights a man who struggled to make laws fair for all people and it opens the door to further discussion about other people in the civil rights movement. In most states, it is also an official holiday. With young children, however, you want to make this holiday meaningful and appropriate for their level of development. Remember that Martin Luther King died when most of their parents or guardians were little, and that's too long ago for three-, four-, and five-year-old children to connect to.

Prepare for this day ahead of time. Commemorate Martin Luther King, Jr., other activists, and the concept of social justice throughout the year, so children don't associate it solely with the holiday. Before the holiday arrives, talk about what "fair" and "unfair" mean. Make a list of children's ideas of unfairness. You will probably get answers such as, when someone teases you, when someone won't hold your hand on the field trip, when everyone gets three crackers and you only get two, or when someone tells you you can't play. Then tell the children that sometimes rules and laws are not fair either. Explain that a long time ago there were some laws that said that people with brown skin couldn't do the same things as people with white skin. People with brown skin had to drink from a separate water fountain, eat at separate restaurants, and go to separate schools; however, many many people worked very hard to change those laws. Martin Luther King, Jr. is one of them.

When the holiday arrives, show a picture of Martin Luther King, Jr. as an adult or read a book such as *Martin Luther King, Jr.: A Picture Story*. Remind children about your discussions about "fair" and "unfair," and tell them that Martin was one of the people who didn't think those laws were fair, so he and a lot of other people who agreed with him tried to get the laws changed. Some children might raise the question of if or how Dr. King died. This may be a sensitive point for some families; however, you won't want to be untruthful when a child asks a question. You may want to discuss this issue with parents and guardians before the day itself. One possibility is to explain in simple language that some people were very mad because they didn't want the laws to be changed. Someone killed Martin by shooting him with a gun. Then reassure the children by letting them know that, even when they want to change things that are unfair, their families, teachers, police officers, and others will work hard to keep them safe.

Remembering Developmentally Appropriate Practice

Good-bye parties and birthdays

Marking important events in children's own lives, such as birthdays and "graduations," with new rituals can make them even more meaningful for individual children. Many programs have developed their own rituals to honor these events. For example, graduation ceremonies bring closure to a year or more of experiences at school or child care and help children prepare for their next step. However, asking children to put on a performance or to sit still while waiting to receive diplomas can be difficult for them. Instead, some programs celebrate the event with a good-bye potluck, where each child prepares and brings in a favorite food to share with the other children and families in his or her group. In one preschool program, the move from the three-year-old to four-year-old classroom is celebrated with a crossing-over ceremony. Teachers place a ribbon between the entrances to the two rooms, and the children symbolically cross over the ribbon to their new class (ReGena Booze, 1992).

Instead of, or in addition to, cupcakes and singing for birthdays, some programs have a ritual at circle time in which the birthday child passes around a pot with soil in it. Each child pushes a seed deep in the soil and makes a wish for the birthday child's upcoming year. The sprouting seeds symbolize wishes that may come to fruition. Another ritual involves reading a special book at circle time that the birthday child's family donates or shares in honor of her or his special day.

Celebrate!

Remembering developmentally appropriate practice will go a long way in helping you change your holiday activities for the better. The next few chapters will help you think more about an anti-bias approach to holidays that validates all children and teaches sensitivity and respect for differences.

CHAPTER **9**

Reflecting All Children

One of the most important considerations when implementing holiday curriculum is that your activities be culturally and individually appropriate for the children in your program. Culturally relevant activities reflect children's home experiences and center on materials, information, and practices that are familiar to children.

Activities That Reflect Home

The most valuable activities are those which mirror children's home lives and accurately portray the way individual families celebrate. Involving children's families as much as possible in planning and implementing your activities will be key to making this work. Participation from parents and guardians makes holiday activities more authentic and more meaningful for everyone involved.

Having most or all of the holiday activities emerge from children and families is a good practice. Instead of planning activities themselves, teachers talk to families who celebrate a particular holiday and invite them to be the source for ideas, materials, and activities. This approach ensures that holiday activities are culturally and individually relevant and reflect individual families' beliefs, perspectives, and customs for particular holidays.

Here are effective ways to involve family members in your activities.

Celebrate!

▶ Encourage families to share information about their holidays and how they celebrate (see chapter 6 for ideas about different methods of communication).

▶ Ask for ideas about what activities would be appropriate to provide for children.

▶ Welcome family members who would like to come in and lead an activity, such as cooking a holiday dish with the children or helping to decorate the classroom.

▶ Request materials that you can use as sources for classroom activities, such as recipes, music tapes, or written words to special holiday songs.

▶ Invite families to loan materials to the program for sharing during circle time. Decorations, children's books, holiday cards, candleholders, and other holiday-related items from families enrich your classroom celebrations.

▶ Communicate to families ahead of time about what you are planning to do in the classroom, so parents or guardians can let you know if they have anything to contribute or any concerns.

Culture Throughout Your Curriculum

Perhaps even more than representing children's and family's holidays in your classroom, it's important to reflect their daily lives. The following are just a few of the many methods to use to ensure that all of your families are represented in your program every day.

● Post pictures of children and their families on your walls.

● Put books on the bookshelf whose characters are of the same culture as your children.

● Keep some "babies" in the dramatic play area whose appearances are similar to the children's in the classroom.

● Talk about the different kinds of family units that are present in your program at circle time. Read books and hang pictures that include the various family units.

● Provide foods for snacks and meals on a daily basis that are similar to what children and families eat at home.

● Include cooking utensils, empty food containers, and articles of clothing in the dramatic play area that come from or reflect those in children's homes.

● Talk to children in their home language.

● When feeding children, putting them to sleep, disciplining, or showing affection, be sure to interact with children in ways that are consistent with how parents or guardians care for them at home.

Work Sensitively With Families

It is critical to be respectful and sensitive when you invite families to participate in your program. Take care to make sure you don't unintentionally offend or alienate a family, or cause them to lose trust in you by making assumptions or acting inconsiderately. Read "Evaluate Your Home/School Relationships" in chapter 3 to check that you have established good communication with families. Then consult books about holidays, talk to people you know who celebrate them, or make use of other resources to gather information before you talk to families. Ask if what you have learned accurately reflects the ways this family practices their holiday and what aspects of it they would be interested in sharing with your group. Remember not to assume that every family who celebrates a holiday does so in the same way.

In addition, remember that holidays can be stressful, especially in December when the pressure is on to buy, buy, buy and to create the extravagant celebrations such as those portrayed in the media. These times can strain families' financial resources and place many demands on their limited time. Be sensitive when you ask families to participate. Avoid asking them to pay for anything if you think financial pressure is an issue. Respect that they may be busy too. A strategy for families under financial or time stresses is to ask for ideas about items that would be appropriate for classroom activities, then borrow or purchase these items and bring them in yourself.

Reflecting All Children

Caution

Be aware that holidays can be a sad and depressing time for some children and families for various reasons, including divorce or the death of a loved one, health concerns, and other stressors. Do your best to support families who are struggling with these issues. Don't make assumptions. Remember that you may or may not know about some of these situations.

Create Balance

Society sends strong messages about which culture's and religion's holidays are considered the most important. Government agencies, banks, schools, and most businesses are closed for Christmas, but not for Hanukkah. They are closed for Thanksgiving, but not for Kwanzaa. We as teachers also give messages to children and families by the amount of emphasis, time, and interest we give to each holiday in our program. An important goal for the implementation of your holiday curriculum is to put equal emphasis on the holidays of all religions and cultures that you present. This will ensure that you convey to children that all their holidays are equally important and valid.

In practice, presenting holidays in an equal, balanced way is particularly difficult for teachers. There are two main reasons. First, we tend to have the most information about (and maybe the most interest in) our own personal holidays. Second, we may have to do some work to find information, materials, and other resources for many holidays that are not of the dominant culture. There is an abundance of decorations, music, videos, children's books, adult books, wrapping paper, cards, and other items for holidays such as Easter, Thanksgiving, Halloween, and Christmas. There are far fewer resources for holidays such as Têt, Diwali, or Ramadan. Also, if the majority of families in the program celebrate one holiday and a small minority celebrates another, then the odds of getting more input, ideas, and resources for the majority's holiday are much greater.

In this situation, it is your job to create a balance that helps all children feel equally validated. These strategies will help you do that.

Do your homework

Fill in the gaps, bring in materials, plan activities, and/or share information about the holidays that are celebrated by only a few children in the program, or that are not represented much in society. Use whatever resources you can find to help you gather enough information and materials to portray these holidays accurately and equally. Talk with families, read books, visit communities where these celebrations take place, visit local community resource centers, and go to libraries.

Help to counter inequalities

You can also help by directly addressing the imbalance in holidays children see around them. This fosters the development of their critical thinking skills. For example, in December, if the children in your program celebrate the dominant culture holidays, you can say, "Sometimes at this time of year people think that everyone celebrates Christmas. But there are many holidays that people celebrate. Not everyone celebrates Christmas" (Kay Taus, 1992). You can continue by explaining to children that "at this time of the year most of the television shows are about Christmas and most of the store decorations are for Christmas, but there are other holidays at this time of the year that seem to get left out, and that makes some people sad."

Don't ignore majority holidays

On the other hand, the answer to balancing holidays in the classroom is *not* to ignore major holidays, such as Christmas, because they get so much attention outside. Christmas is an important and wonderful holiday for many people, and children who celebrate it also deserve validation in their early childhood program. Instead, take a look at other holidays that are just as important

to individuals in your program, and make sure they have an important, equal place in your curriculum.

Avoid Balance Traps

There are three common pitfalls to avoid when trying to create a fair balance among different holidays. In each case, teachers believe they are doing a good job of treating holidays equally, but there are still problems, usually arising from lack of awareness or information. The following are descriptions of the pitfalls and how to avoid them.

Surface-level changes

One trap in balancing holidays is to say that you are doing an inclusive approach when your practices are no different from what you have always done. This often happens in December. A teacher may say that she includes Hanukkah, Christmas, Solstice, and Kwanzaa in her program, and she may be trying hard to do just that. However, a closer look shows that Christmas continues to be the pervasive, most-emphasized holiday. This is what is happening, for example, when a large bulletin board says "Happy Holidays," but the decorations on it include red and green stockings, a cutout paper Santa Claus, decorated paper Christmas trees, and a few snowflakes. Another example is a program that holds its first annual "Holiday Party" instead of the usual "Christmas Party." But the only decorations are a live Christmas tree and a few cut-out dreidels, painted blue and hung on the walls. For entertainment, one of the parents dresses up like Santa and the children sing four songs: "Jingle Bells," "Rudolph," "Silent Night," and "The Dreidel Song." Do you see the problem? What messages are being sent about the importance of these two holidays? What about the other December holidays that aren't mentioned?

To help avoid this trap, examine what you are doing and ask others to help you critique your practices. Then work to equal out imbalances you see and to do a better job of presenting holidays equally.

December-only emphasis

A second balance-related trap in early childhood programs comes from the great emphasis placed on holidays during December. It's true that quite a few holidays fall during this month, and of course Christmas is valued by many people. However, many holidays that are significant to people of other religious or cultural groups happen at other times of the year. Rosh Hashanah and Passover, for example, are two of the most important holidays for many Jewish families. Yet these are often ignored or briefly touched on. Instead, a great emphasis is put on Hanukkah, which usually falls in December, but is not among the most important Jewish holidays.

A solution to this problem is to find out how important a particular holiday is to the people who celebrate it, relative to their other holidays. Then take care to put as much emphasis and excitement into the important holidays you celebrate from January to November as to those you do in December.

Exotic versus "regular" holidays

Even when holidays are given equal time, sometimes one day is treated as "exotic" and another as part of "regular" life (Derman-Sparks, et. al., 1989). This happens often in the "tourist" approach, discussed in chapter 2. Here's an example of the differences between exotic and regular holiday activities. In the classroom where Rosa teaches, many of the children celebrate the American New Year. Don and Cheryl's parents brought in plastic cups, paper plates that said "Happy New Year" on them, balloons, and noisemakers. At circle time, all of the children talked about their wishes for the next year, such as "to be five," "to get a new puppy," "for my daddy to find a job," "to move to a house with a pool," "to get bigger," and "to sleep over at Marissa's house." Afterward, some of the children played pretend "Happy New Year Party" in the dramatic play area.

The next week, because Chinese New Year was approaching, Rosa decided to invite some dancers to come in and do a Lion Dance for the children outside on the playground. Although she didn't know very much about Chinese New Year and didn't have any resources for talking about it with the children, she wanted to expose her children to another kind of new year celebration.

If you have ever seen a Lion Dance you know that it is very colorful, fast paced, and exciting. The children enjoyed the dance and the dancers who were dressed in traditional costumes, although some were afraid of the large, colorful lion's head with the big tongue. But what might they have been learning about Chinese New Year and how it compares to the American New Year they discussed before? As the activities were presented, they might have learned that the American New Year is "regular," an extension of everyday home and classroom life. The Chinese New Year activities, however, although fun and interesting, seemed to portray a message of excitement and difference, a performance by exotic people of their Lion Dance. What could this activity have taught the children in Rosa's class about the Chinese children in their neighborhood, who they are, and what they do at home?

Making some holidays seem exotic is most likely to happen when you are trying to include holidays you have less information about or holidays that no one in the group celebrates. See "Strategies for Including Unfamiliar Holidays" in the next chapter (starting on page 84) for some ideas about appropriately incorporating activities about holidays that you, the children, and their families are unfamliar with.

This issue of presenting holidays equally is one of the tallest hurdles when trying to implement an inclusive, representative approach. It takes perseverance and commitment on your part to create and maintain balance; however, your time is well-spent when your efforts lead to a more equitable and balanced holiday curriculum.

Reflecting All Children

CHAPTER 10

Introducing Unfamiliar Holidays

Using holidays as a primary means for teaching children about cultures with which they have no first-hand connection is a popular but seriously flawed practice. Often, the result is activities that can lead to trivializing and stereotyping cultural groups and have no connection to children's real lives. These have been described as "tourist" activities (Derman-Sparks, et. al., 1989). Still, there are potential benefits to introducing children to cultural groups they are not familiar with, and holidays can be one part of your overall approach. Before you plan activities around holidays that no one in your group celebrates, it's important to think about whether or not this makes sense for your children.

Benefits of including unfamiliar holidays

There are a few good reasons to introduce children to holidays that no one in your program celebrates. One is to help children become a little bit less egocentric and more accepting of holiday practices that are different from their own. Young children tend to think that everyone else does the same things that they do and that their way is the only right way. For children who celebrate majority holidays, this perspective can be compounded by decorations, songs, books, and television programs that permeate society with images of the holidays she

or he celebrates at home. It is wonderful for children to feel pride in and attachment to their family rituals; however, there is also value in helping them learn that many people celebrate holidays that are different from but just as important as their own.

Another reason to introduce unfamiliar holidays is to help prepare children for a world of diversity that they will undoubtedly encounter as they grow. Reinforcing the concept of similarities and differences in as many ways as possible while children are young will help them develop the necessary skills and feelings (such as comfort and empathy) for interacting with the many different people they will meet and experience as adults.

Yet in many cases young children may not be able to learn these skills from holiday activities, because the activities are too complex or too removed from children's daily lives. So how or when will you know whether to include these holidays in your classroom?

Consider Children's Development

The first factor to keep in mind is the developmental stages of the children you teach. Refer back to the chart in chapter 8, page 58, to remind you of how children experience holidays at different ages. Some theorists tell us that there seems to be a developmental shift for children around the ages of five to seven years, when they begin to have a wider and more flexible understanding of different people and different rituals. Because their minds can handle a little bit more abstract thinking at that age, teachers are able to introduce concepts that are more complex than in the preschool years. So, what you can expect to introduce to four-year-old children in a classroom will be very different from what a primary classroom teacher could successfully introduce. For example, third graders can begin to talk about people in other countries, what they wear when celebrating, and what they wear when playing with their friends. They are able to compare and contrast the practices of people in other countries with what they do in their own houses.

Four year olds, however, do not have the ability to think abstractly and reason in the same way. Without some direct experience with the lives of people who live in other countries, preschool-age children are not able to comprehend who these people are or how their lives are similar to or different from their own. They need concrete, first-hand experiences in order to learn and understand.

Consider the Community Context

While keeping in mind the ages and developmental stages of children in your program, also consider the types of communities in which they live. Young children need holiday activities that are similar in some way to their own lives and beliefs, or the lives of people they know. Any holiday activity you share with the children *must* be connected to their experiences in some way.

Do your children live in a racially, ethnically, or culturally diverse community with a lot of exposure to children and families whose beliefs and practices are different from their own? Or do they live in a mostly homogenous area where virtually everyone celebrates the way they do? Considering these questions will help you determine the number of unfamiliar cultural holidays, if any, and how much about a given holiday you can successfully introduce.

If your children live in a diverse area, they will have more concrete experiences with different people to draw on. They are far more likely to have exposure to various holidays, even if they don't celebrate them. Perhaps the Mexican restaurant next door decorates for Cinco de Mayo or the mall down the street has a Kwanzaa celebration. In these communities children often play with neighbors who celebrate differently from themselves or encounter something about other children's holidays while interacting in play groups, dance classes, library storytimes, and so on. As a result, you can introduce a variety of holidays because you can more easily create connections to children's own lives. You will be more limited in terms of how much you can do with unfamiliar cultural holidays if your children live in a homogenous community where everyone comes from a similar background and celebrates like they do, and if there is little opportunity for them to encounter diversity in other areas of their lives. In some ways, children living in these contexts have a greater need for the benefits of being exposed to diversity, but teachers have fewer resources to help create connections and first-hand experiences for these children. Therefore, when using holidays to accomplish this goal, the danger of falling into the trap of a "tourist" approach can be greater. But remember, even in a homogenous community, you will have more success introducing unfamiliar holidays with older children (five years and above) than with younger ones.

Diversity in Homogenous Groups

If the children in your group have little exposure to diversity, the best decision may be to use methods other than holiday activities to broaden their perspective and reinforce the concept of similarities and differences. Here are a few ideas and resources.

Use the diversity that is there

There will be differences in any group of children (or adults), even in seemingly homogeneous groups. Children will look somewhat different, live in a variety of homes, have different family configurations, like to do different things, and celebrate the same holidays differently. Build discussions and activities around these aspects of their lives to talk about similarities and differences. Children's books that are useful

in this effort include *We are All Alike . . . We are All Different* by the Cheltenham Elementary School Kindergartners; *Why am I Different?* by Norma Simon; *Two Eyes, A Nose, and a Mouth* by Roberta Grobel Intrater; *Hats off to Hair* by Virginia Kroll; and *Everybody Cooks Rice* by Norah Dooley.

Read children's literature

Look for stories about characters who are different from your group in appearance or family structure (for example, those who have physical disabilities, darker skin, or live in gay- or lesbian-headed families) but encounter familiar, everyday situations (such as the first day of school or going to the doctor).

Introduce children to persona dolls

Use persona dolls that have different cultural and ethnic backgrounds to tell your group stories about their experiences that your children can relate to. Some of the stories might be about a holiday celebration they had at their "homes" (see "Use Persona Dolls," on page 85, for information).

Use a Diagram to Help You Decide

On pages 82 and 83 there are examples of concentric circle diagrams. This tool can be used to help you decide whether you can include unfamiliar holidays. If you go ahead, they can help you decide which unfamiliar holidays to include based on your children's experiences with diversity. The diagrams illustrate a child's realm of experiences and exposure. The child is in the center and her or his environment radiates out. The people or experiences most familiar to the child appear closest to him or her, and the people or experiences most unfamiliar are farthest away.

There will be different concentric circle diagrams for different programs, depending on many factors such as whether children were born in the United States or another country, and whether they are living in a rural, isolated area or a central, urban area. The following examples are completed diagrams for children in two sample classrooms. The diagram on page 82 reflects children whose families have been in the United States for three or four generations. They have limited experiences out of their state and very little out of the country. The diagram on page 83 represents a different population of children. These children were born in Guatemala, Korea, and Mexico, and are newly arrived in America. Their experiences in other countries are still more familiar to them than those in the United States. Other layers may vary also. Depending on how successful the teachers in their program have been at including elements of the children's daily lives in the classroom, and whether or not the communities that the children live in reflect their ethnic and cultural lives, the layer outside of "other countries" will be either school/center or neighborhood/community. Similarly, if a child regularly visits one of her parents in another state, that state will be familiar and should appear closer to the center.

To make your own diagram, think about your children's experiences. Start from the middle and move out, filling in circles with the names of people or places children are most familiar with and ending with experiences that are the least familiar. You may need to complete more than one diagram if your children come from different types of backgrounds or live in different kinds of communities.

When your diagram or diagrams are complete, review them in light of your children's ages. This will tell you what kinds of holidays they will be able to connect to. As a general rule of thumb, if your children are two years old, they need activities that relate to layers 1, 2, or 3. Threes and fours probably won't gain much from activities outside layer 4 or 5. Fives may benefit from activities up to and including layer 6, depending on their experiences. Six, seven, and eight year olds might enjoy activities that reach out into layer 7 or so.

The diagrams will help you think about how much and what kinds of diversity children are exposed to in their daily lives. This information will help you decide if you should introduce unfamiliar holidays, which holidays those might be, and how much material about that holiday would be appropriate to introduce in your curriculum. Are children's own families diverse? For example, do they live in an interracial family, or have two moms or two dads, or was their grandmother born in another country? How diverse is their school or child care program? Are there children from different backgrounds, and are various languages spoken and/or a variety of religions observed? How about the diversity in the community children live in? What do the store owners and workers look like? What languages do they speak? For older children, you can also think about the level of diversity that exists in the outer layers of their circle.

Celebrate!

Children Whose Families Have Lived in the United States for Three or Four Generations

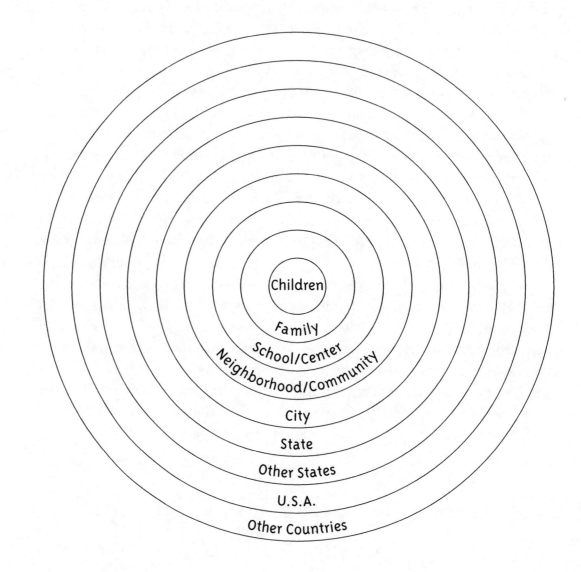

Children

Family

School/Center

Neighborhood/Community

City

State

Other States

U.S.A.

Other Countries

Children Who Have Recently
Moved to the United States

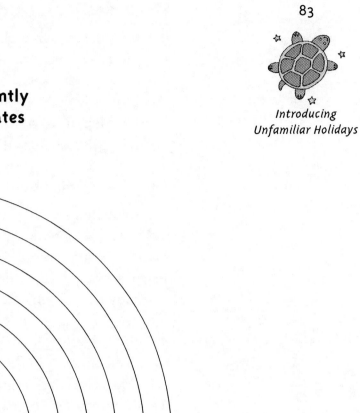

Strategies for Including Unfamiliar Holidays

If you decide that your children are ready to learn about holidays with which they have no direct experience, you must make the connections for them between the holiday and the people or experiences that *are* familiar to them. This way you provide valuable opportunities for exploring similarities and differences without using a "tourist" approach to diversity. Here are some strategies for making connections that other educators have used successfully.

Allow learning about a holiday to emerge naturally

When children are acquainted with individuals from a cultural group other than their own or, for older children, when they learn a lot about the members of a specific cultural group, the holiday practices of the group emerge naturally. Teachers don't have to force them. Here is an example:

Teddy Bear Head Start has four- and five-year-old children from a variety of cultures, including El Salvadorian, Mexican, Japanese, Korean, European American, Native American and African American. There are no Chinese American children in the program and no one who celebrates Chinese New Year. However, the program is situated in a diverse inner-city neighborhood that includes a substantial Chinese American population. Some of the children in the program play with neighbors and friends who are Chinese. Their older siblings attend school with children who are Chinese American.

Every January in this community there is a huge Chinese New Year celebration, including a parade that passes in front of Teddy Bear Head Start. Learning about Chinese New Year in the classroom seems natural, because it is an important holiday in the community where the program is located and where many children live, and the children have some understanding of who Chinese people are. Teachers can introduce the holiday in a meaningful way because they know that their discussions about this holiday won't be the first time children learn anything about people who are Chinese or Chinese American.

Talk to a class friend

If there is someone who regularly visits your classroom and who celebrates a holiday that is new to children, invite her or him to share it with the group. The visitor might be a librarian, public health nurse, teacher trainer, custodian, diaper delivery person, Spanish teacher, supervisor or director, and so on. It is important for children to know the person well, before she or he is asked to speak about a holiday. The children need to connect to the individual first before they can connect to the person's holiday in a meaningful way (Sharon Cronin, 1992).

Share your own holidays

If you celebrate a holiday that your children do not, your explanation of the holiday and how you experience it provides a concrete way for children to understand it. Sharing this part of yourself will also allow the children to connect with you in a new, more personal way.

Use persona dolls

One of the most effective ways to tell stories to children is through persona dolls. These are dolls whose physical characteristics include any of a variety of skin colors and features. Some persona dolls also have physical disabilities. In the classroom, these dolls have distinct personas that never change. The dolls come out at various times and the children eventually learn all about them, almost as if they were additional members of the classroom. The children also learn about each doll's special holidays as they come up, just as they would with anyone else in the classroom.

For example, "Katherine" is a persona doll with light brown skin, long, light brown hair, and almond-shaped eyes. Her "mother" is European American, and her "father" is Japanese American. Katherine's "grandfather," who is ill, lives at her house and has a nurse who takes care of him during the day while her parents work. "Katherine" visits the classroom on many occasions so her teacher can tell a story about something that happened to her, which is very similar to something that happened to a child in the class. Sometimes these are everyday stories, such as helping children solve an issue that arose in the sandbox. Sometimes it is a more personal story about her feelings or experiences at home. The beauty of persona dolls is that you can supplement what actually happens in the classroom through the "experiences" of the dolls. Below is an example of a persona doll who shares an unfamiliar holiday with the children in one teacher's classroom.

Sample Persona Doll Story: "Thomas Celebrates Solstice"

When I brought a persona doll named Thomas to circle time in the preschool room, the children welcomed their friend to the group with enthusiasm. Several children yelled "Yea, Thomas is here!" Thomas had visited the children a few times prior. The visit they remember the most was when he came to the group with Lauren, another doll, because the two of them had a problem. Thomas always wanted to play with Lauren, just Lauren and no one else. Lauren liked Thomas but was annoyed that he always followed her around and wanted to play with only her. I brought the dolls and the problem to the group because a similar, real life situation was happening in the preschool room. I presented the problem and asked the children to brainstorm ways

that Lauren and Thomas could solve it. This time, however, I brought Thomas to the group on December 23 to tell the children about how Thomas celebrates Solstice. I began the story . . .

"Thomas came to visit you today because he wants to tell you about a special holiday that he celebrates with his family. We've been talking a lot about holidays lately. Last week we talked about Hanukkah and how some of you celebrate Hanukkah at your homes, and now we're talking about Christmas. There are other holidays at this time of the year and one of them is called Solstice. This is a holiday that Thomas celebrates at his house. He brought a special book with him today that he wants me to read to you about Solstice. The book is called *Dear Rebecca, Winter is Here.*"

Then I read the book, which simply and concretely talks about the changes in the seasons. When I finished reading the book, I explained a little bit more about Solstice.

"Solstice is a time of year when some people celebrate the fact that the days are getting longer and the sun is starting to stay out longer. Remember when the days started getting shorter and it started getting dark right after snack time, before your moms or dads picked you up? Well, soon after Solstice, the days will start getting longer again, and soon it will be light out when your moms and dads pick you up. Some people think this is very important and like to celebrate it. At Thomas' house they celebrate it by decorating a tree outside in their front yard with food for the birds and squirrels. They hang up peanut butter bird-feeders, popcorn string, and other treats that animals like. They also light candles in their house to celebrate the sun and the light that starts to come back after Solstice."

After this discussion I explained to the children that Thomas was inviting them to make candleholders with him today in honor of Solstice. After circle time the children joined Thomas at the art table and had a great time molding and decorating clay candleholders for the candles they chose.

✳ ✳ ✳ ✳ ✳ ✳ ✳ ✳ ✳ ✳ ✳ ✳ ✳ ✳ ✳ ✳ ✳

Connect unfamiliar holidays to familiar ones

One way to make the connection for children is to focus on the underlying themes that many holidays have in common, such as festivals of light or liberation. Children are able to identify more successfully with a holiday and the people who celebrate it when the new celebration has a theme similar to their own. Here are some examples of common themes and a sampling of holidays associated with them.

▶ **Liberation:** Fourth of July, Mexican Independence Day, Passover, Hanukkah, Cinco de Mayo, Juneteenth (the 19th of June, 1865, was the day when slaves in Texas learned they were free), and Martin Luther King, Jr.'s Birthday

- ▶ **Harvest:** Thanksgiving, Kwanzaa (African American harvest celebration), Sukkot (Jewish harvest festival), Makahiki (Hawaiian harvest)

- ▶ **New Year:** American New Year's Day, Rosh Hashanah (Jewish New Year), Chinese New Year, Hmong New Year, Tết (Vietnamese New Year) (Note that almost all cultures have a new year celebration. This is just a sampling.)

- ▶ **Death:** Dia de Los Muertos (Mexican Day of the Dead), Kwanzaa, All Souls Day, Memorial Day

- ▶ **Festivals of Light:** Christmas, Hanukkah, Kwanzaa, Santa Lucia Day (Swedish light festival), Diwali (Hindu festival of lights)

There are many ways to make the connections among holidays for children. One way is simply to explain the connection in age-appropriate language. You might say, "Remember when we talked about the holiday called the Fourth of July? Remember that we talked about it being a liberation celebration because it was the birth of the United States? Well, we're going to talk about another holiday that is a liberation celebration, and that is called Hanukkah. Some people who are Jewish celebrate Hanukkah because it reminds them of a long time ago when Jewish people fought to take something back that was theirs. They fought to take back their temple which had been taken away from them" (ReGena Booze, 1992).

The festival of light theme can then be exemplified in activities that celebrate light. For example, teachers at the child care program at Pacific Oaks Children's School have invented a candle group ritual that takes place during the winter months, when the days get shorter and the October, November, December, and January holidays emerge. The children make candleholders to hold their own special candle, and every day at around 5:30 P.M., half an hour before the center closes for the day, the children all gather on the carpet for "Candle Group." The safety rules about candles are reviewed, the candles are lit, and the lights are dimmed. Children are invited to sing peaceful songs related to the holidays, the time of the year, liberation struggles, or anything else that comes to mind. They know that this is a special ritual saved for the time of the year when the days grow shorter and when the holidays that relate to light (Solstice, Kwanzaa, Hanukkah, Christmas, Diwali, Santa Lucia Day, and others) are around the corner.

Weave aspects of different holidays into your program year-round

Keep holiday books on the book shelves all year so children and teachers can have conversations throughout the year about particular holidays and the values they put forth. Let relevant decorations stay up on the walls. For example, good

luck symbols from Chinese New Year and a poster of the Nguzo Saba (Seven Principles of Kwanzaa) commemorate principles that can be incorporated into the curriculum all year. Through repetition and connection to daily events, the holidays and the meanings that underlie them become more familiar.

Here's an example of how this works. The seven principles of Kwanzaa are Umoja (unity), Kujichagulia (self-determination), Ujima (working together), Ujamaa (cooperative economics), Nia (purpose), Kuumba (creativity), and Imani (faith). You might choose to make the principles of working together, creativity, and faith (having confidence in ourselves) year-round themes in your classroom, well before the holiday begins. As you talk about these principles, they will come to have meaning for your children, and in turn, the holiday that celebrates them will become more meaningful. When Kwanzaa comes around in December, you can remind children that you've been talking about the important messages of the Nguzo Saba all year long (ReGena Booze, 1992).

Points to Remember

Whatever strategies you use for introducing unfamiliar cultural holidays, keep these important points in mind.

- Activities about a holiday should never be children's first introduction to or last mention of a cultural group. Children must first have an understanding of who people are and how they live their daily lives, so they can build a context in which to comprehend a holiday or celebration. Without this context, information about a holiday may seem too different from their own experience and too difficult to understand. As a result, children may form stereotypes about the "strange" people who celebrate this "different" holiday.

- Focus on the feelings people have when they celebrate their special holiday or engage in a family ritual. Feelings are real for young children and something they can connect to and identify with, especially if the feeling is related to one they've had before. Be careful not to extract external pieces of a holiday, such as food or dress, without the feeling component.

- When you implement activities from other people's holidays, you run the risk of doing them inappropriately. Make sure you do your research and gather sufficient information about the holiday so that you don't give children any misinformation or perpetuate stereotypes. A visit to the communities of people who celebrate the holiday can offer you a lot of information. You can also use the library, children's books, individuals in the community, and cultural centers for information.

Deciding about whether and how to include unfamiliar holidays in your classroom is an important piece of implementing an anti-bias approach to holidays. The issues may seem complicated, but with planning and forethought, and evaluating your activities afterwards, you will make the best decisions for your program.

CHAPTER **11**

Addressing Stereotypes and Commercialism

Unfortunately, many of our national holidays contain stereotypical images and messages, or present history from only one perspective; others are heavily influenced by commercial interests which equate celebrating with buying.

Young children are strongly influenced by messages which surround them. They may take stereotypical images as correct and true information about other groups or even about themselves. They may feel their holidays or families are not as good as others if their home celebrations don't live up to the images on television.

As part of our commitment to help children develop to their fullest potential, caregivers have a responsibility to help them recognize and reject these unfair images and messages. By actively talking about and, in some cases, taking action against stereotypes and mass commercialism, we encourage the development of critical thinking and empowerment in the children and families we work with. We protect the self-esteem and self-image of children in our programs who are threatened by these messages, and we help children gain accurate information about people who are different from themselves, as well as develop skills for interacting with others.

Caution

Acknowledging that a holiday includes stereotypes does not mean you have to or should avoid it altogether. These holidays have positive, worthwhile aspects and some or all of them may be important to the children and families in your classroom. By addressing the stereotypes in these holidays, you allow their underlying, positive values or messages to shine through.

Understand Stereotypes

Stereotypes are hurtful because they demean and dehumanize individuals and groups, perpetuate prejudices, and teach misinformation. They are not only damaging to the people stereotyped, but also to every child who will grow up with false information about history and who will absorb inaccurate and hurtful information about the lives of others. The following are prevalent examples of stereotypes in our national holidays.

Columbus Day

Columbus Day retells only the European side of the historic event it commemorates and ignores the Native American perspective. It gives misinformation by saying Europeans "discovered" America, when there were thousands of people and vibrant cultures already here. These people were often enslaved or killed by the invaders, their land was stolen, and the diseases the Europeans brought with them killed entire tribes.

Halloween

Halloween brings with it some hurtful images and messages. The color black is portrayed as bad and evil through black cats, black bats, and black witches' costumes. Senior women are portrayed as green-faced, wart-nosed evil beings. Both of these images leave lasting impressions with children and shape their ideas about people. For example, it is very common for young children to be afraid of elderly women. When asked why, they will often say because "she looks like a witch." Similarly, the negative portrayal of the color black (which persists year-round in images and phrases such as black-clothed villains, black sheep, devil's food cake, and blacklist, to name just a few) affects children's feelings about things that are black. It also affects their attitudes about people who are African American (Black).

Thanksgiving

Like Columbus Day, Thanksgiving tells a story from the perspective of the European settlers and leaves out the story of Native Americans. What is generally portrayed as a time of friendship, neighborliness, and thankfulness was in fact the beginning of lost land, broken promises, diseases, and death for many Native Peoples.

Another problem with Thanksgiving is that it brings out, in abundance, stereotypical images of Native Americans. These people are portrayed inaccurately and hurtfully as half-naked, uncivilized, grunting individuals. Greeting cards and decorations are also abundant, some with pictures of animals dressed up as Indians (and Pilgrims), images that are dehumanizing and disrespectful.

Caution

It is hurtful and disrespectful to allow children who aren't Native American to wear "Indian" costumes for a holiday celebration or at any time. Cultural identity is something people are born with and a large part of who they are. Dressing up to be "Indians" is offensive, just as it would be to dress up to be "African Americans" or "Italian Americans." In the proper context, it can be appropriate for children to dress up to play the role of a particular individual (such as Martin Luther King or Rosa Parks in the Montgomery Bus Boycott). Of course, it is appropriate for children to use costumes to play out occupations, such as mommies or train engineers, but it is *not* acceptable for them to dress as an "at large" member of a cultural group.

Researching stereotypes is a good way to help you understand more about them. It is important to explore and investigate why certain holidays are offensive to some people. You can start investigating by yourself or with colleagues. Use resources listed at the back of this book, such as: "Why I'm Not Thankful for Thanksgiving" by Michael Dorris; "Beyond Ten Little Indians and Turkeys" by Patricia Ramsey; *Encounter* by Jane Yolen; *A People's History of the United States* by Howard Zinn; *Anti-Bias Curriculum: Tools for Empowering Young Children* by Louise Derman-Sparks et al.; and *Through Indian Eyes* by Beverly Slapin and Doris Seale.

These and other resources may also help you identify your own possible biases. Challenge yourself to identify which stereotypical messages you personally have absorbed. What did you learn from holidays in school and in the media when you were a child? Spend some time talking with your co-workers, a support group of concerned teachers or parents and guardians, anti-bias educators, or your supervisor about stereotypes in holidays before you address them with children. Work on raising your awareness first, before you go any further.

Celebrate!

Address Holiday Stereotypes in Your Classroom

Addressing stereotypes in effective, age-appropriate ways takes attention and advance planning. The information and support you gather will help you examine your holiday ideas and activities for potential stereotypes and bias. Evaluate your plans, then think about how you will proceed. Here are strategies to help you on your way.

Consider the developmental levels of your children

Before you can begin to counter stereotypes with your children, you must be sure they are ready. You'll have the most success getting your message across if children are at least three or four years old. At this point children are really absorbing the negative images and messages from holidays and other media, and they are ready to talk about them.

One way to find out if children are developmentally ready to talk about stereotypes in holidays is to interview them. Their responses will help you know what to do next. For example, sit down with children at circle time and ask "What are you learning about Indians?" (You may have to use this term instead of "Native Americans" at first.) If the children have no response or respond in unconnected ways that don't really answer the question, they may not be ready. However, if you get responses such as, "They kill people, they don't wear shoes or underwear, they dance around a fire and go 'woo, woo, woo'," then you know they are picking up negative messages and it's time to undo some of what's been done.

Help children gain accurate information

Children need accurate information about what people really look like, how they really feel, and what events really happened in history to help them counter stereotypes. Provide them with developmentally appropriate information. Give them time to process it and answer their questions simply and honestly. For example, explain to children that stories about and pictures of mean, ugly witches make some senior women feel sad. Sometimes children who read these books and see these pictures think that all women who are old enough to be grandmothers are mean witches. It hurts older women's feelings when children are afraid to talk with them, hug them, or hold their hands because they think the women are bad witches.

There are also quite a few good books available today that depict accurate, current images of Native Americans. Reading these books and talking about the pictures of Native people in their daily lives is another way to dispel some myths and address stereotypes.

Encourage children to think critically about stereotypic images

During holidays, point out to children that "there are pictures (or messages or stories) about this holiday that are not fair" (Louise Derman-Sparks, 1992). Over time, children can learn to look at images and ask themselves if they see anything that is unfair or hurtful to people. This question can expand their already growing sense of "fair and unfair" and help build their cultural sensitivity.

Adding something to the children's environment or bringing in a book is one way to start a conversation about images that are unfair. For example, many teachers have developed a collection of stereotypical Thanksgiving cards and wall decorations. Bring these in and compare and contrast them with photos of real Native Americans living today. Talk with the children about how the cards and wall decorations might make people who are Native American feel. You might also use a persona doll that is Native American to talk about feeling sad at Thanksgiving and to explain that her or his family doesn't celebrate this holiday and why.

Make cultural respect, sensitivity, and fairness a year-long theme

Avoid the trap of talking about groups only around a holiday that stereotypes them (for example, older women in October or Native Americans in November). This is another form of the "tourist" approach, where people are discussed only in terms of holidays. Instead, help children learn about people from various cultural groups all year long. Focus on their day to day lives and ways that these are similar to or different from the every day lives of your children. This way, talking about a group and how they are misrepresented or stereotyped in a holiday is only one of the meaningful conversations you have about them during the year.

Talk With Families

Include discussions about stereotypes in your ongoing communication with families about holidays, well before a holiday arrives. Share with families' information (written, verbal, or both) about hurtful messages and images. Explain to them how you plan to address the issue with children, and ask for their ideas and feedback.

Consider holding a meeting with parents and guardians to talk further about your concerns and your planned approach. Get the support of your director or local expert to help you explain the issues involved. Remember that some families may feel sad, angry, or defensive if the holiday you are talking about is one that they celebrate. *Emphasize that you will not negate everything about the holiday, but will celebrate the positive aspects with children.* To help them understand the importance of addressing these issues, be sure to point out that absorbing negative

messages about cultural groups hurt all children, those who belong to the groups being stereotyped and those who don't. These messages can negatively affect children's growing self-esteem and self-identities, and impair the skills they are developing for understanding and interacting with people who are different from them.

Address Commercialism

The overemphasis on buying things at holiday time is frustrating to many people. It minimizes the real story or message of holidays and focuses instead on what to purchase to make you and your family happier. This emphasis can also put unnecessary pressure on families with limited financial resources and can make children whose holiday celebrations feature fewer things feel inferior.

Some holidays seem to have been taken over by commercialism and business marketing strategies. Valentine's Day, Halloween, Thanksgiving, Christmas, Easter, and St. Patrick's Day are clear examples. Hanukkah is beginning to be effected as well. Reflect on your goals for holidays and your overall classroom goals for children. If your goals include validating children's experiences, making holiday activities fun and enjoyable, or promoting connectedness among children and families, it will be important for you to counter commercialism and materialism. Here are some strategies to try.

Talk with children about the underlying messages of individual holidays

Focus children's attention on the meanings behind holidays. Tell them a little bit about the historical story of the holiday if they are older than three or four. For example, explain that Thanksgiving is a day for being thankful for the things we have and the people we care about, or that people celebrate Christmas to remember when a very special baby named Jesus was born many, many years ago.

Explain the symbolism behind the decorations children see around them

Shiny red hearts, shamrocks, Easter eggs and bunnies, jack-o'-lanterns, turkeys, and Christmas trees permeate children's environments during their respective seasons. Simple, concrete information about their meanings will help children put the holiday and its purpose in perspective.

Remind children that holidays are also times for thinking about others

Provide opportunities for children to create homemade gifts for people they love or people in need. This is appropriate during December or any time. Remember to avoid teacher-directed crafts; rather, provide open-ended materials that allow children's creative juices to flow.

Help children think critically about television commercials and other advertising

Explain to children that these forms of media are trying to encourage them to buy certain food and toys so companies can make money. (For more information about the media and the advertising industry's effects on children, see *Who's Calling the Shots? How to Respond Effectively to Children's Fascination with War Play and War Toys* by Levin and Carlsson-Paige.)

Help children develop realistic expectations about gifts

Talk with families about what their children's expectations should be, and ask how they would like you to reinforce these. This may be particularly important if the families in your program can't afford or don't choose to provide the kind of holidays portrayed in the media and some books. One way to handle this is to remind the child about her or his family's practices. You might say to a child, for example, "At your house, you get one big present and one little present. That's the way it is at your house. At other people's houses it's different. Some people get no presents because they don't celebrate Hanukkah or Christmas or any other holiday at this time of year. And some people get a lot of presents. You celebrate Christmas, and on Christmas morning, you get one big present and one little present."

Counter the message that having more means being valued more

The media has done a good job of reinforcing the story that Santa only brings presents to good girls and boys. Sadly, this damaging story can lead children to think they are bad if they receive few or no presents. Here's a possible response if you run into this situation. "I believe that all children are good. I don't think that being bad or good is what causes you to get presents or not. I think that children get presents in lots of different ways because people celebrate different holidays in different ways. Some children celebrate Christmas and get a lot of presents on Christmas morning. Some children celebrate Christmas and get a few presents on Christmas Eve. Some children don't get any presents. Some children don't celebrate Christmas at all. But none of that means children are good or bad." At the same time, be careful not to undermine any family's wish

that their child continue to believe in magical or mystical beings like Santa Claus or St. Nick.

Respond to Families' Circumstances

A common, difficult situation you might encounter is discovering that a child whose family celebrates a holiday, such as Christmas, doesn't have the financial means to buy any presents. If appropriate, talk to the family about this. Ask what words the parents or guardians use to explain the situation to their child. If they need ideas, brainstorm possible ways that they or you can talk about this with the individual child. Work with your colleagues or your supervisor to come up with strategies for responding to questions from other children who do get presents about why this child doesn't get any. Also ask your director or supervisor if your program has developed strategies for helping families in financial need by referring them to agencies and programs that donate goods and gifts, or by participating in a gift donation program at the school or center. Treat this issue with respect and sensitivity.

Help Children Stand Up to Bias

With the support of families and teachers, children can learn to take action against unfair images or messages they see during holidays. As you uncover with children the stereotypes in holidays, it is also important to give them tools for doing something about them. Here are some tools that encourage children to take action against hurtfulness.

Write letters

Invite children to send letters to card companies or stores telling them how they feel about hurtful cards, decorations, pins, or buttons for holidays such as Thanksgiving or Halloween. Children can also suggest alternative ideas for these products. Have the children dictate what they want you to write, then they can all sign their names to the letter.

Modify stories

Help children suggest new words for books about Columbus' "discovery" of the Americas that tell a more accurate story and include the perspectives of the people who were already living here. Insert new sentences or paragraphs into existing books about Columbus, or write your own classroom book with the children.

Help children talk to families

Support children in explaining to their families what they've learned about how "Indian" Halloween costumes hurt the feelings of people who are Native American, and how witch costumes teach unfair things about senior women.

Send home an article for families that further describes the problems. You might try the material in chapter 10 in *Anti-Bias Curriculum: Tools for Empowering Young Children* by L. Derman-Sparks, et al.; chapter 5 in *Teaching and Learning in a Diverse World* by Patricia Ramsey; chapter 6 in *Roots and Wings* by Stacey York; and "Why I'm Not Thankful for Thanksgiving" by Michael Dorris.

Whatever activities you use, it's important to support and acknowledge children each time they point out something that is unfair in holiday images. Help empower them by asking if they would like to do something about it.

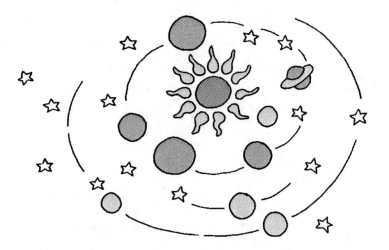

CHAPTER **12**

Considering Religion

It is important to give special care and attention to the religious aspects of holidays in your curriculum. Most holidays, including many of the national holidays, have strong religious components to them. One of your most challenging and important jobs will be to handle religion in ways that respect families' beliefs, without going against the constitutional guarantee of the separation of church and state, and without trivializing holidays by losing the essence of their meaning or focusing on their commercial representations.

There are many issues to consider when making decisions about religion. Here are some steps to help you find answers for your program.

Consider Your Own Perspective

You are on a holiday journey that requires constant introspection and self-reflection. Religion is a part of culture and has a strong impact on the way people see the world and on their daily lives. (This is true even if you choose not to practice a religion.) Yet, just as it was important to put aside your personal feelings about holidays in general, you need to be able to separate from your work with children your own religious beliefs and any biases that you might have about other beliefs. Your most important job is to meet the needs of all the children in your care, those whose religion is similar to yours and those whose religion is different. Remember that supporting and respecting a child's and

102

Celebrate!

family's beliefs doesn't necessarily mean you agree with them, but such support is essential in helping each child develop to her or his fullest potential.

To be able to provide this support, you must understand your own strong feelings and beliefs about religion. Ask yourself the questions in the box below. Challenge yourself to honestly explore what your feelings are regarding religion in the classroom. Meet with colleagues or your director or supervisor to discuss your thoughts.

What Are Your Thoughts About Religion?

Ask yourself the following questions to get in touch with your own feelings and beliefs.

- Do you consider yourself a religious or spiritual person?
- How important is your religion or spirituality to you?
- What place do you feel religion has in the classroom?
- How comfortable do you feel talking about the beliefs of other religions?
- Do you think teaching religious values is the teacher's job?
  The family's job? Both?

Don't be surprised if you react personally to matters of religion. It is a foundation for some people. It's easy to become sensitive or defensive if a practice you believe in is challenged or omitted from the curriculum. It is common to have that reaction, but be sure to think before deciding if and how to respond. Another common response for teachers who are struggling to become more sensitive regarding religious issues is to go to an extreme in the other direction, becoming highly critical of the beliefs and practices of their own religion. While it is good to be aware, it won't necessarily help you or the children you work with to negate your own strongly held beliefs.

Monitor Your Responses

Once you've done the initial checking-in with your feelings, your ongoing task is to examine your comments and reactions to issues as they come up. Do you show respect for other beliefs? Can children sense that you are uncomfortable if they talk about God? Think about some potential responses you can give to children so that you are not taken by surprise when children ask questions about religion. Practice your answers with a co-worker or your supervisor. Strive to be accepting and inclusive in all your comments.

Identify Your Program Type

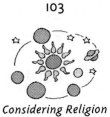

Take a close look at the nature of your program. Your program type will set the parameters for the decisions you can make about religion.

Public schools

All early childhood programs that receive public funding and/or are affiliated with any public organizations must comply with the First Amendment of the Constitution of the United States, which guarantees the separation of church and state. The principle of separation was created to ensure that the government could not dictate what religion is right for everyone. It guarantees religious freedom and the right of people to choose. So if you work in a public school program, or one that is funded by the federal or state government, such as Head Start or a state university laboratory school, you are legally restricted in the degree to which you can incorporate religion in your classroom. (If you are not sure how your program is funded, now is the time to find out.) When teachers in a public program invite children to pray when lighting Hanukkah candles or to sing Christmas carols, they blur the roles of church and state and may be contradicting the First Amendment.

However, there is wide variation in the way that administrators and teachers define the separation of church and state. For example, in some programs teachers cannot mention holiday names such as Christmas or Hanukkah, and must use the words "holiday" or "winter" to refer to anything related to December celebrations. There is a "winter party," "holiday music," "holiday cards," and a "winter break." In other programs, it is acceptable to talk about Santa Claus and Christmas trees but not Jesus.

Some teachers feel it is okay to talk about religion if children bring it up first. Others say it is never allowable to talk about religious stories or teachings. These educators believe teachers should just defer to children's parents or guardians when a child asks a question about religion. There is a constant debate over how far teachers can go. If you teach in a publicly funded program, be sure you know what your program's regulations are and what guidelines the administration has set forth before going further.

Religious-based schools

If your program is affiliated with a church, temple, mosque, or other religious entity, then you have a whole different set of considerations. If your program has clear goals and rules about what religions and what aspects of religion should be included, your job is a little bit easier. In most Jewish programs, for example, it is usually expected that all of the major Jewish holidays will be observed. This is not something teachers have to seek approval for from parents and guardians or co-workers. Instead, it is generally spelled out in the program's

mission statement and in the written policies and procedures that families receive when they enroll their children and that staff receive when they are hired.

What is a little bit harder to decide in a religious-based program, however, is whether or not to include holidays that are not specific to the religion to which the program adheres. There is a wide range of approaches. In some programs, holidays from other religions and cultural groups might not be celebrated per se, but they may be mentioned and a little bit of information about them may be shared with children. In other programs, the holidays of other religions are not mentioned at all.

Private, non-sectarian schools

If yours is a private program that has no relationship to a public agency or a religious entity and does not receive public moneys, then you have more freedom legally to include the religious aspects of holidays. Making decisions about religion can actually be more difficult here. When the separation of church and state doesn't apply and the focus of the program isn't on a particular religion, the possibilities are endless.

Consult Your Program's Philosophy

Whatever your program type, your individual program may already have a written philosophy in place regarding religion. A written philosophy can give you guidelines for answering children's questions about God(s) and religious and spiritual issues. It also guides approaches to curriculum and what kinds of material purchases can be made (such as children's books), making clear what practices are acceptable and what to avoid. Check your written policies and procedures, especially the staff or parent/guardian handbooks for your program. It certainly makes your work easier if there is already a policy in place. If your program doesn't have a policy about religion, perhaps it is time to gather with staff and the administration to write one.

Reflect on Your Goals

The type of program you work in will also influence your goals for children regarding religious holidays. Think about your goals within the context of your program. Are they:

- ▶ to teach the values of a specific religion?
- ▶ to validate children's familiar cultural experiences?
- ▶ to help children understand that there is vast diversity in what and how people celebrate?

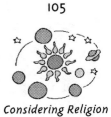

- to help children understand the importance of religion in some people's lives?

- to teach children a little bit about the religions of the children and families in the program?

Your answers to these questions will influence your practices.

Work With Families

You need to work closely with families as you decide if, when, and how to talk to children about the religious aspects of holidays. This information will be an important guide as you plan activities and discussions. If your program already has a policy in place on how religion is generally handled, make sure you review that before speaking with families. You can review the section titled "Evaluate Your Home/School Relationships" in chapter 3, and "Select Your Methods" in chapter 6, to gain ideas for communicating with families. The sample family questionnaire about holidays on page 43 shows one way to give information and solicit feedback. Other strategies listed there will be useful as well, such as talking to families individually or bringing up the topic during a home visit.

As you discuss religion with families, you may discover that some families in your program object to your including religion in holiday activities or discussions at all. Others may be concerned that one religion is going to be put forth as the "right" one. Still others may be very excited about the idea of their child being exposed to the religious stories and beliefs inherent in holiday celebrations. Listen carefully to all of the families' concerns and preferences. Balance their input with your own philosophies as an educator and with the parameters set by your program. Discuss the options with your colleagues and director or supervisor, and make the best decisions for your program. Then, with help from your colleagues or supervisor, explain the decision you reached after considering how best to meet the needs of the families and children and to accomplish your holiday goals in the classroom. Inform families about what's happening in the classroom regarding religious activities or discussions on an ongoing basis. Invite them to talk with you if they have questions or concerns, as you hope they would with any area of curriculum.

When Families Disagree

If some families in the room differ on what they want to see happen in the curriculum, encourage dialogue among those families at a parent/guardian meeting that you or your director or supervisor facilitate. Hopefully, together you can arrive at a solution that meets everyone's needs. But if some families prefer an approach that is very different from the one you decide to use, talk to them about the situation. Tell them what you can and can't do, and why.

Celebrate!

Explain in what ways you believe your approach will meet their child's individual needs. (If they still don't agree, see the next chapter for ideas about modifying your program to meet families' objections, and strategies to use when a compromise can't be reached.)

Choose Your Approach

So, what are strategies for handling holidays that include religion? They fall into two broad categories, avoiding religion or including it, with many variations within each.

Avoiding Religion

Steering away from the topic of religion may be a good option for you if your program is publicly funded or if, for other reasons, you and your colleagues prefer to minimize religious discussion in your classroom. But in practice, avoiding religion can be difficult because it is such an elemental part of many holidays. It can also cause some problems. If you treat a religious holiday as a purely cultural or historic event, you run the risk of diminishing and trivializing the core meaning for those who celebrate it. For example, to most Christians, Christmas is not only about Santa Claus and evergreens, and Jesus is not simply a man who lived two thousand years ago and taught specific doctrines. For them, Christmas celebrates the birth of Christ, who was and is God in human form, a powerful, life-sustaining deity. To some, presenting Christmas is meaningless without acknowledging this aspect of it.

Still, avoiding religion may be the best approach for your program, and many teachers have successfully presented meaningful holiday activities without a religious component. Here are some strategies.

STRESS CULTURAL ASPECTS

When telling children what a holiday is about, downplay the religious story and symbols and stress only the cultural parts of the holiday. When the topic of religion comes up, acknowledge that many families celebrate the religious story in this holiday, then gently refer children to their own families for information. For example, if a child wants to know more about God, tell her "let's talk to your dad about this when he picks you up today." At pick-up time, help the child explain her question to her father.

EMPHASIZE UNDERLYING VALUES

Talk about the values of love, care, connection, joy of life, sense of wonder, awe, trust, thankfulness, and/or hope that are a part of many religions and their holidays, without directly talking about religious stories. For example, many Native American celebrations honor the Great Spirit. Spirituality is an elemental component of these celebrations and observances. However, it is possible to highlight values such as family, connections, and thankfulness, which are important parts of the beliefs and activities tied to celebrations, without going into discussion about the Great Spirit. For example, a Cherokee stomp dance is like a prayer to those who participate, and it is a spiritual celebration. However, when a child in the group is talking about the singing and dancing that he took part in at a summer stomp dance, you can support him as he describes the feelings of sharing and togetherness he experienced, and avoid talking about the spiritual aspects.

HIGHLIGHT UNDERLYING THEMES

A useful strategy that was mentioned earlier in this book is to focus on the themes or seasonal aspects of holidays, and thereby avoid discussions about religion. For example, some teachers have had success focusing on the theme of "Festival of Lights" during the winter holidays and avoiding extensive individual activities about Las Posadas, Christmas, Kwanzaa, Hanukkah, Diwali, or Solstice. Within this approach, having a winter festival party can meet the needs of families and staff members who want to celebrate together during the winter months, but want to avoid religious discussion in their child care program. (If you choose this option, make sure your party isn't just a Christmas program under a different name. See "Avoid Balance Traps," page 73, for thoughts on this.)

DISCUSS INSTEAD OF CELEBRATE

This is a another good general strategy for holiday activities that also works well for religion. For example, you might have a child in your program who celebrates Las Posadas, a Mexican holiday that falls on December 16. She could share with the children at circle time about how her family and other families in her neighborhood celebrated the holiday by reenacting Joseph and Mary's search for an inn where Mary could give birth to Jesus. But don't follow up with activities such as having children act out this procession in the classroom.

When you invite family members to come in and talk about their holiday, ask them not to discuss the religious belief system behind it. For example, someone from a Muslim family may talk to children about Ramadan and explain how during this holiday adults (and sometimes children) don't eat or drink anything until the sun goes down. However, the information that Ramadan commemorates Allah's first revelations to Muhammad can be left out.

REDIRECT CHILDREN'S DISCUSSIONS

Often children raise the topic of religion. For example, a child may want to talk about his or her experiences going to church at Easter. Because it is important to honor and validate children's experiences outside the classroom, that is okay. However, if someone wants to talk about God or what the priest said about God, you might say, "Yes, some families believe that. People believe lots of different

things about God. At home, you and your family can talk a lot about God and what you believe." Then redirect the discussion by asking the child what else she/he did over the weekend (Roberta Hunter, 1992).

Including Religion

An alternative approach to minimizing religion is to deal directly with the religious aspects of holidays. Of course, this is only an option for religious or private, non-sectarian programs. In non-sectarian programs, it is difficult to find a way to include the religious aspects of holidays that doesn't concern, offend, or ostracize anyone. But many teachers believe it is a necessity. They argue that children need this information about holidays and that to avoid giving it is to risk diminishing the significance and the truths of the meaning behind the holidays. Others feel strongly that religion is a part of children's cultures and identities, a critical part for some children. If part of our job as teachers is to validate children, they ask, how can we avoid religion?

Figuring out a sensitive approach to including religion is a challenging—and ongoing—process, but it can be done. Here are ideas that other teachers have used successfully.

TELL THE RELIGIOUS STORY

Plan ahead of time how you will tell the religious story of the holiday at circle time or during an activity. Having a plan will ensure that you have thought carefully about how to share the information in sensitive and age-appropriate ways. Your goal is to let children know a little about the ways that some people who are a part of the class celebrate a particular day, and that other people acknowledge the same holiday in different ways. Here are some examples:

- When talking about Diwali, the Hindu festival of lights, you might explain to children that "On this holiday some people who are Hindu put candles outside their door to help Rama, one of their gods, find his way home."

- A way to talk about Christmas is to tell children "This is the day that some people celebrate as Jesus' birthday." To explain who Jesus is, you might say "Jesus was a baby who grew up to be a leader. He is very important to people who are Christians."

- When talking about a Native American powwow, explain that prayers are sometimes said at the beginning and end of the powwows.

FOCUS ON FAMILY'S BELIEFS

Center your discussions on the ways the families in your program teach and practice the religious aspects of their holidays. Ask families to come in and talk about their beliefs in simple, developmentally appropriate ways. Invite parents or guardians to bring in an object or perform part of a ritual that children can observe.

Another, straightforward approach is to let questions about religion emerge from the children, then answer them directly and matter-of-factly. You will still have to plan ahead so you are prepared to answer questions accurately, but this approach ensures that children only get information they are asking for.

Considering Religion

Points to Remember

As you know, the issue of religion in an early childhood program is very sensitive. To make sure you are doing the best job you can, remember these essential points.

1. Keeping discussions and activities about religious holidays developmentally appropriate can be especially challenging, because the stories, values, and messages of different religions can be particularly abstract and difficult for young children to understand. Make sure that your discussions and activities about religion do not frighten, confuse, or frustrate children; make sure they are meaningful and understandable. Use simple, straightforward language. See the paragraph entitled "Tell the religious story, " page 108, for examples of how to talk to children about the religious aspects of holidays. Whenever possible, bring in or borrow objects that relate to the holiday to give children something concrete to see and hold.

2. Tread very carefully when talking about religions or religious beliefs. Defer to children and their families for information about their religions and what they believe. This is especially important for religious beliefs different from your own; however, even among people who practice the same faith, you still may find some differences.

3. It is extremely important to use the words "some people" when talking to children about the beliefs and practices of a particular religion (ReGena Booze, 1992). For example, "Some people believe that . . ." or "On this holiday, some people . . . ." Educators must be careful not to put forth any religious belief or practice as the one that *everyone* in the class believes in and participates in. (In some religious programs it may be appropriate to do this, but religious-based programs in which there are some children of other religions must be sensitive to these differences.)

4. A fine line exists between talking about a holiday that has a strong religious component and teaching the religion. For example, Christmas carols like "Joy to the World," which refers to Jesus as the Lord and the earth's king, are religious and, some would say, teach the values of the Christian religion. Similarly, be sure to avoid activities that might teach religion, unless that is your intended goal. If a child or family member wants to re-create in the classroom a ritual that they practice at home, help the other children understand that they are "guests." Observing and discussing rituals is more appropriate for children than participating if the rituals aren't ones that their families practice or believe in.

Celebrate!

Consider Issues of Diversity

Chapter 10 discussed the question of whether to bring unfamiliar cultural holidays into your classroom. It is particularly important to think carefully about this question when holidays have a strong religious component, because of the possibility of being inaccurate or offensive. In general, the guidelines for making this decision are the same for religious holidays as they are for others. Review the steps in chapter 10 to help you decide. Then, if you do choose to include an unfamiliar religious holiday, use the strategies there for help in implementing them appropriately in your classroom.

Some teachers fall into the trap of bringing religious activities into the classroom without realizing that that is what they are doing. This is especially true for Native American religious rituals. Activities such as sand painting, creating a drum circle, burning sage, and using and wearing feathers are all sacred, spiritual rituals in Native American groups. There is a certain protocol for these rituals and how they occur with regard to the roles of men and women, who can participate, and what the rituals mean. To re-create them in the classroom with the intent of participating in a "Native American activity" is inappropriate and offensive unless the activity is led by a Native American child or her or his family. This would be similar to holding Christian communion in the classroom.

Another common problem arises around the issue of balance. As discussed in the previous chapter, it is important to treat religion and religious holidays in consistent ways. For example, if you tell the religious story of one holiday, be sure you are able to tell the religious stories of other holidays with equal accuracy and depth. If you are not able to do this, you convey to children that the story you know is the one that is important. In fact, some educators believe you should not tell children which religion (if any) you adhere to, because as their teacher you have so much influence on their developing values and attitudes (Bill Sparks, 1992). If you aren't familiar with the religious story behind a particular holiday, find someone who can give you the necessary information before you talk about it with the children.

Also be aware of your degrees of comfort or discomfort with different religious holidays, and make sure you approach them consistently in the classroom. For example, if you are introducing discussions and activities around the religious aspects of Passover, which celebrates the time long ago when Moses led the Jews out of slavery, don't limit your Easter activities to eggs and bunnies because you are uncomfortable talking about Jesus.

Refer constantly and consistently to your goals for holidays as you venture forward planning and implementing holidays activities. Don't worry about making mistakes. They are inevitable. Just be willing to be self-reflective and constantly evaluate your practices (see chapter 7 for information about evaluating activities).

CHAPTER **13**

Meeting Needs When Families Don't Celebrate

Occasionally there may be children and families in your program who don't celebrate any holidays, due to religious or other reasons. Families who are Jehovah's Witnesses, for example, typically don't celebrate any birthdays or holidays. In other cases, families may celebrate generally, but may not want their child to take part in a particular holiday. For example, a Jewish family may accept the majority of holiday activities in the classroom, but feel very strongly that they don't want their child to participate in Christmas activities such as singing carols in a performance. A Muslim family may not want their child exposed to any activities related to Easter. Christian families may not want their child to participate in Halloween activities. Another family that is uncomfortable with political activism may object to their child participating in a neighborhood peace march in observance of Veterans Day.

This can present a challenging situation for you, especially if holidays and holiday activities are the foundation of your curriculum. But a commitment to fairness, respect, and inclusion means finding viable approaches that meet the needs of every child and family. Depending on your situation, the approaches can range from modifying your activities somewhat so families are comfortable with them, to eliminating one or all holidays entirely from your program.

Celebrate!

However, if you work in a program where holiday activities are a central part of your curriculum, such as a religion-based program, you may not have the option to eliminate holidays. In this case, especially if holidays make up a large part of your curriculum, your program will probably not be a good fit for a family who doesn't celebrate holidays. You or your director should review your holiday practices and policies with the family and help them make that decision.

The steps in this chapter will help you find solutions that meet the needs of the many different families who don't celebrate any holidays, as well as those families who don't want their child to participate in particular holidays.

Examine Your Own Feelings

As in other questions about holidays, your personal feelings and beliefs can be a strong influence when it comes to families who don't celebrate. For some of us, holidays were the highlights of our childhoods and continue to be an important part of our adult lives. If this is the case for you, you may feel sorry for the child whose family beliefs or values prohibits her or him from celebrating all or specific holidays. You may feel that this child is missing out because she or he won't experience presents or Santa Claus at Christmas, or baskets and colored eggs at Easter. You may feel, too, that a child is being deprived if she or he doesn't have birthday parties. You may also want to share your own excitement about and enjoyment of the holidays with the children you work with. However, the children's needs may be different from yours.

Some teachers see families that don't participate in celebrations as "inconvenient" for upsetting their holiday curriculum plans. This is often the case in classrooms where the majority of the children and families do celebrate and want holiday activities to appear in the curriculum. In this situation it is not uncommon for caregivers to feel anger toward the family who doesn't celebrate and become concerned about how to meet the needs of "all the other children" when "just one child" isn't allowed to take part.

If you find yourself having these thoughts or feelings, get in touch with whatever might be behind them *before* you start the process of finding solutions. Remember that your job as a caregiver is to help each and every child develop to her or his fullest potential. Remember, too, that the goal in the celebration of similarities and differences is to include *all* children. Your commitment to and reaffirmation of these goals is important. Try looking at this challenge as another opportunity to make your classroom a fairer place, one where all ways of living are celebrated.

Dialogue With Families

Remember that families may not want their children to participate in specific holidays for a variety of reasons. Whenever a holiday is approaching that you suspect some of the families don't celebrate, or if you think or know that some of your families don't celebrate any holidays, take the time to find out from each family if they are comfortable with the activities you are planning. Let families who do not want their child to participate in this (or any) holiday activity know that you would like to work closely with them to make sure you meet their child's needs. Consider talking with your director or supervisor to gain some support and get ideas for working with the family who doesn't want their child to participate. Then approach the family. There are many communication methods you can choose from. If you generally hold parent/guardian conferences in your classroom, consider setting up a meeting as soon as possible to talk about this issue. If you are more accustomed to sending home a letter and asking for a response, try that. If you do home visits, you might discuss this topic then. Or you may feel most comfortable talking informally, perhaps when families drop off or pick up their child. (If you use this approach and the child is nearby, show consideration by including her or him in the conversation.) Whatever approach you use, start the dialogue *before* the holiday is about to begin.

Meeting Needs When Families Don't Celebrate

Provide Information

When you talk with families, describe your program's approach to holidays. Begin by giving examples of the types of classroom holiday activities you have done in the past. Provide as much detailed information as possible so the family has a good idea of your approach. For example, explain to families that when you talk with children about holidays, you always make it clear that "some families" believe in and celebrate these ideas and "some" don't. Tell them that you base holiday activities on the ways individual children in your classroom celebrate. If you are in a non-sectarian program, assure them that you do not present one religion as the "right" one. Share examples of specific holiday activities as well, such as making cards as an activity choice for Valentine's Day. Describe the materials that are available—various colors of construction paper, doilies, stickers, and crayons—and explain that some children opt to make valentine cards for friends and families while others do not. If the family enters the program in the middle of the year, share with them the holiday plans you have in place for the rest of the year. As you do, explain that many of these activities are negotiable and that you will make changes to meet their family's needs.

Ask Questions

The next step is to gather specific information from the family about what is acceptable to them and what isn't. Don't assume you know, even if you know something about the family's background or know another family from the same background. Give this family an opportunity to share with you their individual perspective on holidays and what experiences they want their child to have or not have in your classroom. At the same time, it will help you to earn the family's trust if you have a little knowledge about their background before you speak with them. A good approach may be to talk to other people or read books about the religious or cultural group the family belongs to. Then ask families if this information is a true reflection of what their family believes and practices.

Ask the families some specific questions to further clarify their practices and wishes. For example, if the family is Jehovah's Witness, you might ask: Should all celebrations be avoided or only ones with a religious basis? Can your child participate in social justice holidays like Martin Luther King, Jr.'s Birthday? Are invented celebrations acceptable, such as Backwards Day or end of the year celebrations to say good-bye to graduating children? Is it okay for your child to be present in the classroom when holiday activities are going on? If so, can she or he participate in any way? For example, if another parent or guardian brings in a treat to share for a child's birthday, can your child participate? Can she sing "Happy Birthday," or eat the snack? (See the Resource section of this book for helpful books about the Jehovah's Witness religion.)

As you talk with different families, you may discover that there is variation about what celebrations and activities are acceptable. For some Jehovah's Witnesses, it is acceptable for children to make a pine tree out of construction paper but not to decorate it. Or they may be allowed to make a pumpkin as long as it doesn't have any facial features. For other Witness families, a Thanksgiving celebration may not be allowed, but they may welcome their child's participation in a Harvest Party, where the emphasis is on sharing and preparing good foods and learning how we get these foods from nature (Jane Davis Stone, 1991). For still other families, any activity related to a holiday in any way may be too much.

Be sure to listen thoughtfully. Keep an open mind toward all of the information the family shares with you. Building trust and gaining the family's respect will be of utmost importance as you work with them and other families throughout the year. Work hard at understanding the perspective of these families and letting go temporarily of your own strong feelings.

Recheck Your Emotions

If your practice has been to base much of your curriculum on holidays, you may feel now that you will have to significantly change your approach, and yet your efforts may still not be enough for families who don't want their child to participate in any holiday activities at all. It is hard not to get defensive when this situation arises. Learn all you can and then take some time afterward to work through whatever feelings come up for you, such as anger or frustration, with a co-teacher, director, or a colleague in the field but outside of your program. In the long run you will realize that because of the changes you make, your overall curriculum will be more reflective and inclusive of all children and families in your classroom.

Caution

Remember that it is not your job to try to persuade families to raise their child differently. Instead, it is your role to value, respect, and support individual families' child-rearing practices. Think about it this way. Hopefully you wouldn't try to convince a family of vegetarians to begin eating meat (Jane Davis Stone, 1991) or try to sway a Christian parent to become Jewish. Your role should be one of support, acceptance, understanding, and cooperation. Use this situation as another opportunity to talk about the different ways families can be.

Provide Different Options

When you have an idea of a family's needs, take responsibility for playing a role in finding a solution. It is not fair to expect the family who doesn't want their child to participate to come up with all of the answers. Instead, brainstorm some possible solutions on your own or with your colleagues. You may find that you need to alter your practices just a bit in order to make the activities acceptable to all families. The following strategies, also described in earlier chapters, may offer solutions for families who don't celebrate.

RECOGNIZE INSTEAD OF CELEBRATE

Sometimes approaches that teach children about a holiday without asking them to participate in it are acceptable to families who don't celebrate that holiday. This may mean limiting your holiday activities to discussions, reading books, and having family members talk about how they celebrate at home.

OFFER MANY ACTIVITY CHOICES

For some families, just knowing that their child won't be forced to participate in a holiday activity, or be made to feel ostracized for not doing so, may be all that's required. In that case, making holiday activities a choice instead of a whole-group or required activity may be the answer. Provide enough interesting options so a child who can not participate in the holiday activity can easily choose another. All that child may need is a gentle reminder to choose one of

the other activities. It is also helpful to make activities open-ended, so that children can use the materials in any way they choose. Then, for example, while some children are decorating paper bag Halloween costumes, a child who doesn't celebrate Halloween can decorate a paper bag mural or a paper bag puppet.

Caution

When providing alternative activities for children who can't participate in a particular holiday, remember that the alternatives which are offered should be equally as enjoyable as any holiday activities. Also, if something is made an option for one child, it should be made an option for every child. That way one child doesn't feel excluded or bad for not engaging in holiday activities that everyone else is doing.

❦ AVOID RELIGION

For some families, avoiding discussion about the religious aspects of holidays and focusing on the cultural aspects may meet their needs. As mentioned in chapter 12, this is difficult to do because religion is an intrinsic part of many holidays. However, it is possible to de-emphasize religious discussion and avoid religious symbols and still talk about a particular holiday. Be sure to check with the families in your classroom to find out what parts of holidays they consider to be religious and what you'll need to avoid.

❦ CHANGE YOUR FOCUS

Altering your approach to an activity is another possibility. If, for example, the activity that a family has the most trouble with is birthday parties, request that families save birthday celebrations for home. Then implement another activity in lieu of birthday celebrations. One idea is to have VIP days. Each child, on his or her VIP day, gets the spotlight. A variety of pictures of the child and his or her family go up on the bulletin board, along with information about favorite colors, favorite animals, a drawing of where the child lives, and a story written by the child. Similarly, if there is a child in the program whose family doesn't want her or him to participate in any activities related to Halloween, ask families to help you come up with a viable alternative. One avenue might be to focus on the themes of harvest or masquerade instead of Halloween.

❦ CONSIDER OMITTING HOLIDAYS THAT ARE PARTICULARLY PROBLEMATIC

If you discover that one holiday is particularly problematic for many families in the program, it is appropriate to weigh the pros and cons of omitting it from the curriculum. Situations where this approach may be a good option include a program with many Christian families who object strongly to the celebration of Halloween, or a program with many Native American families who don't want their child to participate in traditional Thanksgiving activities. Consider this approach, too, if even just one or two families strongly object to a particular holiday. Since your goal is to meet the needs of each and every child, as well as the needs of the whole group, think carefully about which practice will be best. Consider talking this over with colleagues and your director or supervisor to get ideas and support before making any decisions.

HONOR FAMILIES' REQUESTS THAT THE CHILD NOT BE PRESENT

A final option is for a child to be removed from the room (or stay at home) when holiday activities are going on. This should be a very last resort and a solution that the family proposes rather than the teacher. In some cases, however, this may be the only feasible choice if families do not want their child to be present during activities that are holiday related in any way, and holidays will still be included in the program. If you use this approach, make sure the child who is being removed, and the children who aren't, understand that this isn't a punishment for the child who can't participate in the activity. For example, if you go for a walk with a child, invite other classmates to come along so all children realize they can choose whether or not to participate (ReGena Booze, 1992).

Communicate With Other Families

If you think it's appropriate, talk with all families about the adjustments you are making in your holiday curriculum to accommodate families who don't celebrate. In some cases you might want to include other families in deciding what changes to make. Remind families that, as part of your commitment to being an individualized program, the curriculum needs to be fair and meet the needs of each and every child. Explain that all families may have to yield some of their wishes in order to enhance your program's culture of fairness and inclusiveness. Keep in mind, however, that your role in this situation can be tricky. It is up to you to ensure that the family who doesn't celebrate (especially if there is just one) isn't made to feel like a nuisance because of their values or beliefs. Do not allow other families to make them feel that way. Remind parents or guardians that you modify classroom practices and make decisions based on individual children on a regular basis. Help families see this situation as a valuable learning opportunity for their child and for themselves.

Support Children

It is important to work with all of the children, those who celebrate and those who don't, to help them appreciate and respect each other's family practices. Children who celebrate national holidays get great validation from stories, television shows, and other aspects of society. Due to children's egocentric nature,

Celebrate!

it is easy for them to think that what they do is "right." They might even think that another child is bad, sad, or unloved when his or her family doesn't participate in holidays at home. These children need help to understand that there is nothing "wrong" with a child or family who doesn't celebrate.

Equally or even more important, children who don't celebrate holidays get little or no validation for their practices from our larger society. It is your job to help these children feel validated, supported, and welcomed in your classroom.

Working with families, you can also help children who don't celebrate holidays develop strategies for living in a society where holidays play a large role. Encourage families who don't celebrate holidays to help prepare their child for a classroom of children who do. Suggest that families give children words to help them explain why they do not participate in certain activities at school (Jane Davis Stone, 1991). Find out what those words are so you can support the child and family. Also ask the parents or guardians to talk to their child about the kinds of activities they will find at school during the holidays. Questions may arise at that time that families can answer better than teachers.

Try these strategies for supporting and educating all children around the issue of families who don't celebrate.

Bring in a persona doll

Use a doll at circle time to "talk" to your group about why its "family" doesn't celebrate a specific holiday or any holidays. The doll can also talk about what it's like to work on different activities, leave the room, or stay home while others are participating in holiday activities. This is a good technique for giving children who celebrate simple, concrete information about the beliefs and practices of families who don't. It also helps them to understand what children who don't celebrate holidays might be feeling. For the children who don't celebrate, having a persona doll with a similar identity can relieve some feelings of isolation and some of the pressure to do all of the explaining about her family's beliefs. This is especially important if there is only one child in the class who doesn't celebrate. (See chapter 10, and Derman-Sparks, et al., 1989, for more information on using persona dolls.)

Find a book — or write one

If a child in your program belongs to a religion that doesn't celebrate holidays, look for good, sensitive books about other children who belong to this religion too. If you are unable to find such a book, make your own. Create a main character who has enough in common with your children so they can identify with her, and who follows the same religious practices as your child who doesn't celebrate. Maybe the child in your book loves to go to school and enjoys soccer, T-ball, and cupcakes; however, birthday parties are hard for her because everyone else gets to eat cupcakes, but she has to wait until the celebration is over to eat hers. Then the character can explain why she can't participate in the birthday parties at school.

Invite family members

You might invite a family member who doesn't celebrate holidays to come in and share with the group something fun that their family does together. This gives other children an opportunity to learn that while their classmate and his or her family don't celebrate holidays, they do enjoy fun things together. They might not celebrate birthdays, but they might exchange presents at other times of the year, take trips to places like the circus and the zoo, and in some families, have a special family dinner together every week. They are not sad, solemn families that never laugh. At the same time, having a family member come into the classroom gives the child who doesn't celebrate an important opportunity to be recognized and validated for his or her family and something they do at home.

CHAPTER 14

Michael's, Sheryl's, and Margery's Classrooms

While all early childhood teachers will take similar steps to define their approach to holidays, holiday practices will ultimately vary widely from program to program. In this chapter are three stories set in three different early childhood settings. The stories describe the children and families that make up the program, and how each program handles holidays. They are told from the perspective of the teachers that work in the program. The teachers and the names of the programs are fictitious, but the holiday practices described are ones used in real-life programs.

"Michael's Story"

Michael teaches three year olds in a classroom at Dandelion Child Care Center. This center is a private, nonprofit, non-sectarian child care program that serves children ages two months to five years. It is entirely funded by tuition.

The children who attend Dandelion are mostly European American, with a few African American and a few Asian American children. Almost all of the children come from middle to upper middle-class families, except for a few children whose tuition is subsidized by the city. There are a variety of religious beliefs represented, including Christian, Jewish, and Muslim. Some of the families are also Jehovah's Witnesses.

Celebrate!

Approach to holidays

Holidays are a fairly significant part of the program. I include about two or three holidays in the curriculum each month.

Goals

I make sure that the holidays of the children in the program have a very important place in the curriculum. I feel it is important to validate the children and families' identities and beliefs, and to recognize that what they do at home together is very important to them. At the same time, I know that for the Christian children, whose holidays are represented everywhere in the media, stores, cards, and decorations, it is particularly important to learn that there are other holidays celebrated in the world that are just as valid and important as those that they celebrate.

Choosing holidays

I put together a list of holidays, starting with what children and families in the program celebrate, as well as what I celebrate. I learn about what and how families celebrate by sending out questionnaires. I include the holidays that I celebrate personally because this is a natural extension of the children's relationship with me. They spend five days with me every week. Learning about the days and events that are important to me is something they are interested in. I think it makes me seem more "regular" to them, especially when what I celebrate or the way I do it is similar to their practices. Then I include a few other holidays because I really want to expand awareness of and comfort with differences among this fairly homogeneous group. To make sure children have some real-life connection with these holidays, I choose ones that are celebrated in the surrounding community.

This year, the holidays that the children and families in the program celebrate are the American New Year, Martin Luther King, Jr.'s Birthday, Chinese New Year, Valentine's Day, St. Patrick's Day, Easter, Passover, Fourth of July, Rosh Hashanah, Halloween, Ramadan, Id ul-Fitr—which celebrates the end of the fasting during Ramadan—Thanksgiving, Hanukkah, Christmas, and Mother's and Father's Days. We celebrate these last two as "Family Day" because that is more inclusive and respects the different family configurations we have in our program. One of the holidays I celebrate that I will share with the children is Solstice. The community holidays I'll bring in include Dia de Los Muertos (Day of the Dead) and Kwanzaa.

Implementation

Holiday activities in our classroom can be as simple as reading a book about a holiday and as elaborate and involved as having a party in the classroom, with food, decorations, guests, and music. In most cases, however, holidays are more recognized than celebrated. Our activities usually involve a short group discussion about a holiday and how a family celebrates it, or we'll read a book about a holiday.

Occasionally I will set up developmentally appropriate activities for children that relate to a holiday. These activities are usually centered on the way a family in the program celebrates at home. For example, in October and November many of the children in my classroom have pumpkins in their homes, so we often experiment with pumpkins during that time. I cut open a pumpkin and put it in the sensory table so children can touch the flesh, feel the coolness inside, separate the seeds from the pumpkin, and experience the smell of fresh pumpkin. Later, we rinse and dry the seeds and bake them, like many children have done or will do at home. Sometimes family members will come in and take part in an activity with us. One year the children and I designed jack-o'-lantern faces, and I helped a parent cut them out.

Although less common, there will occasionally be a party to celebrate a holiday. This usually happens when families really want a party. For example, if some children's older siblings are having a Halloween or Valentine's Day party in grade school, families sometimes want their preschoolers to have one too. The family members do the planning. They will bring in a special treat and maybe some napkins and paper cups, and we'll sing and have a little party. I just ask them to keep it fairly low key, so the children don't get over stimulated.

Because of the age group of the children in my classroom, oftentimes I talk about holidays after they've occurred instead of before. The holidays are fresher in children's minds then and the discussions are more meaningful to them. I've tried to ask children what their family did for a particular holiday last year, and generally they just don't remember. But when we come back to school on January 2, after a short winter break, some of the children want to talk about how they had a New Year party at their house and Grandma or Auntie came over for dinner.

I often tie holidays together by their common themes. I've found that this works really well for my three year olds, who need to hear the same concepts repeated over and over again. I use this approach to introduce holidays that are present in the community but not celebrated by families in the classroom. For example, many children in the program celebrate Christmas and Hanukkah. We talk about the common theme of light in both holidays; there are lights on the Christmas tree, lights on the advent wreath, lights on the menorah. This paves the way for understanding something about Kwanzaa and Solstice, because there are lights on the Kwanzaa kinara, and Solstice is all about the return of light (the sun) as the days get longer again. Throughout this time, we experiment with flashlights, make candleholders out of clay, and eat lunch and nap by candlelight. One day last year a parent brought in a menorah and I brought

in a kinara (candleholder for Kwanzaa), and we lit both during nap time. The older threes have really latched on to this idea of Christmas, Hanukkah, Solstice, and Kwanzaa all being festivals of light. I can point out that while they are celebrating Christmas, Hanukkah, or both, other people are celebrating Kwanzaa or Solstice, holidays that are similar to but different from theirs.

Religion

Since Dandelion is a private program, we have lots of leeway with religion. In my classroom I have chosen to actively tell the religious stories that go with holidays. The director is very supportive of this approach. Of course, this has to be done very simply with threes, and I am very careful to give concrete, non-biased information. I use the words "some people" when I talk about religion so that children begin to learn that not everyone believes in the same religious stories or the same religion. For example, I will say, "Some people, people who are Christians, believe in Jesus. On Christmas, people who believe in Jesus celebrate his birthday because they are so happy he was born." Then, to make it concrete for children, I'll say, "At Sally's house, this is what they believe and they go to church on Christmas to celebrate Jesus' birthday." Similarly, to explain Ramadan, I tell children that people who are Muslim celebrate this day to remember their God, Allah, and his follower, Muhammed. I also explain that during Ramadan, adults and some children fast (that means they only eat after the sun goes down and before it comes up in the morning). I work very closely with families on the issue of religion. I explain to them ahead of time how I will talk about the religious aspects of holidays and give them time to give me feedback. I always refer children back to their parents if they ask for more information.

Working with Families

In our school, families are fairly involved. We have bi-monthly family meetings on a variety of topics, and a policy that requires family members to participate in the program in some way at least one hour every month. I also communicate with parents and guardians regularly, especially at the end of the day, about their child and how the day was.

At the beginning of each year I send out questionnaires asking for a lot of information, including information about holidays. Then I invite families to a meeting on this topic. I describe how I tend to handle holidays, and I invite family members to help make decisions about what and how we'll celebrate during the coming year. We'll talk about developmentally appropriate practices and the need to tailor all activities to the developmental levels of three year olds. I remind families that, at this age, children will need lots of hands-on activities that stimulate their senses. They will relate the most to short books, short discussions, and activities from their own and other's homes. I'll also take the opportunity at a meeting to ask families for information about their own holidays, especially if I haven't yet gotten back their questionnaires. Then I get together with parents and guardians on a regular basis, at least once a year, to assess how our holiday practices have been working and where we can improve.

Throughout the process, I work to build trust with families. I want them to be involved with this part of the curriculum as much as possible. I also want to involve families in my efforts to make sure there is equality among the holidays presented.

Working with children who don't celebrate

I do have two families in the classroom who are Jehovah's Witnesses and don't celebrate holidays. This has been a real challenge for me, but one that I've welcomed. I've used it as a series of teachable moments, another way to talk about differences and similarities. One of the families tends to be flexible about what their daughter can participate in. She is able to be present in the classroom when we are discussing a holiday, because we are usually just reading a book or talking about it. I always make sure to tell her mom about every single activity I am planning so she has some time to talk with me about it before it happens. Many times the child can participate in the activities I plan because I present them in a way that is acceptable to her mother. For example, I always set up all of my activities as a choice, so no one, including this child, ever has to participate if they don't want to. They can just choose one of the other activities.

The other family in my classroom seems to be more strict. Whenever we are doing an actual holiday-related activity, the child and I, and any other children who want to, leave the room. For example, in the fall a parent came in to cut out jack-o'-lanterns with the children. Before they got started, I went for a walk to the library with the child who couldn't participate, and Amy, my assistant, stayed in the classroom with the director. On the way to the library, I explained to the child that her mom and dad thought it might be too hard for her to be in the classroom right now because some kids are cutting out jack-o'-lanterns and her parents don't want her to. While we're gone, Amy explains to the other children why this child left the room. She uses this opportunity to teach about religious diversity. Amy will say something to the children like, "Some families believe in making jack-o'-lanterns and some don't. It depends on your religious beliefs and what your family wants you to do." In general the parents of this child have been pleased with our efforts to meet their needs and to not ostracize them or their child. I am careful not to disapprove of them, and I do not treat them like they are depriving their child because they don't celebrate birthdays or holidays.

Celebrate!

"Sheryl's Story"

Sheryl teaches four and five year olds in a classroom at Spruce Street Head Start. As a Head Start, Spruce Street is public, non-sectarian, and receives its funding from the federal government.

The children who go to Spruce Street are from many racial and ethnic backgrounds including Latino (El Salvadorian, Guatemalan, Mexican), African American, Asian American (Chinese American, Japanese American, Korean American), a small population of Native Americans (Anishinabe/Ojibway), and a few who are European American. The majority of the families are Christian, although there are some Muslim, Hindu, and Buddhist families as well. All the children come from low-income families.

Approach to holidays

Holidays are a consistent part of the curriculum but a small part. We don't have many parties, but we do some activities and have discussions. I often use holidays to highlight classroom themes.

Goals

My biggest goal is to validate the children's and families' experiences. Many of the children in my classroom celebrate holidays that they don't see reflected in society at large, so I want them to see them here. Since parents and guardians are involved in Head Start, when they bring in holiday recipes or books or decorations, it helps to make that home-school connection. I also want children to learn about each other's holidays, and I want them to recognize unfairness and take action to change it when they can.

Choosing holidays

I talk about most of the holidays that are celebrated by children and families in the program, even if they are religious. I just try not to focus on the religious aspects. I tend not to talk about any holidays that the families in the classroom don't celebrate because there is already so much diversity here. I can easily meet my goal of exposing children to holidays other than their own without bringing in any additional holidays.

Holidays that are included this year are Las Posadas, Christmas, Kwanzaa, Hanukkah, Chinese New Year, Japanese New Year, Korean New Year, Hindu New Year, Martin Luther King, Jr.'s Birthday, Black History Month, Valentine's Day, Hana Matsuri (Japanese Buddhist Flower Festival), Easter, Ramadan, Anishinabe Thanksgiving for the Maple Trees, Juneteenth (June 19, 1865, was when slaves in Texas learned they were free; this holiday is celebrated by some of our African American families from the South), Mexican Independence Day, Halloween, Dia de Los Muertos, and Thanksgiving.

Implementation

I try to pick out the underlying, nonreligious values of holidays and focus on those. For Valentine's Day we focus on the giving as well as the receiving of valentines. We talk a lot about what it means to be a friend and how you show somebody that you care about them. We also talk about how great it feels to give cards to people we care about. We usually read a book at circle time about friendship, and then, during activity time, I set out a whole array of materials that children can use to make valentines. I try to steer away from commercial influences and provide open-ended materials that are interesting to children—folded construction paper, doilies, glitter, sequins, beads, buttons, stamps, stickers, and cut-out pictures from magazines that reflect their cultural groups. Children can make whatever they'd like with the materials. If they make a card for a friend or family member, that's great. If they don't, that's okay too. For Martin Luther King, Jr.'s Birthday, we highlight the conversations about fairness that we have all year long. We talk about it not being fair when someone ruins your block structure, tells you that you can't play, or says you talk funny. I explain to them that Martin Luther King and many other people wanted to make things more fair for everyone. We make signs about fairness, whatever the children want to say, and then march through the school with our signs.

I also look for similar underlying values and messages in holidays to make connections for children. For example, for American New Year, I usually talk a little bit with children, maybe interview them about what they know about the holiday, and write down their words. Then we will talk a little bit about "out with the old and in with the new." Sometimes we wash babies and clean up the classroom. I talk about the other new year's celebrations represented in the classroom, too, like Korean, Japanese, and Hindu New Year. Depending on what the children celebrate at home, I go more into the idea of "cleansing for a new beginning," because that is an important theme of many new year holidays. I point out similarities and differences with other holidays to connect these new year celebrations with ones that children are familiar with. Some of our children are still learning English, so our conversations are usually short and simple. In addition, I tie together Juneteenth, Mexican Independence Day, and Black History Month because they all have similar themes of activism and fighting for fairness.

We talk a lot throughout the year about the issues these holidays bring up, then use the holidays to underscore these important ideas. For example, fairness and changing things that aren't fair is an ongoing topic for us. We talk about how a long time ago people who were African American were slaves. That meant they worked for white people, doing anything they were told to do. Many people, both African Americans and white people, thought that wasn't fair. We talk about Harriet Tubman, John Brown, Frederick Douglass, the

Michael's, Sheryl's and Margery's Classrooms

Grimke sisters, and others who helped African Americans become free. When June 19 (Juneteenth) comes along, we talk about how this was the day that African Americans who lived in Texas learned they were free. To give them a frame of reference, we look at a map together, and I point out how far away Texas is from where the children in the program live. Depending on the group of children, I might also talk about how long after January 1 (Emancipation Day) June 19 is and how the African Americans in Texas had to be slaves for so much longer than other slaves.

Another technique I use is having persona dolls "tell" stories about holidays. I often tell the stories in small groups to make communication easier. Because the dolls are such a powerful teaching tool, it really gets the children's attention and helps them connect to the holidays and the people who celebrate them. It also keeps the focus off the one or two children that might celebrate a particular holiday, so they don't feel too different from everyone else. Sometimes that's a concern of families in my classroom. They don't want their children to feel too different. They want them to feel "American" and to fit in. I let them know that I will work hard to help them fit in and feel comfortable, but that I also want to celebrate their identity and their cultural background. I'm teaching the parents and guardians how to use the persona dolls, too, so they can tell stories in their native language.

Religion

Though our curriculum includes religious holidays that the children celebrate, religion can be a challenging issue for us because, as a Head Start, we don't do any religious teaching. Since we receive federal money, we have to abide by the separation of church and state. So in activities and discussions, I avoid the religious aspects as much as possible.

This year we will talk about Las Posadas, but it's going to be hard to avoid religion in this case because traditionally this holiday involves reenacting Joseph and Mary's journey as they look for an inn where Mary can give birth. Children usually take part in the dramatization. I will probably invite a family to talk a little bit about how they celebrate, and leave it at that. If children ask me about who Joseph and Mary are I'll say something like, "If you are Christian, you probably believe that Mary was Jesus' mother and Joseph was Mary's husband."

If children want to know more about a religious belief or story, I'll refer them to their families. I do that regularly when children ask questions about religion. I don't want to just cut them off, because I don't want them to get the message that something is wrong with asking questions or with religion itself. For example, a child once asked me if God was real. I responded by asking, "What do you think?" He didn't answer, so I explained, "Teachers here will not tell you about what is true and what's not true about God. Your family and whatever church, mosque, synagogue, or temple you go to is where you will get that answer." Then I am careful to tell children's families about these conversations, so they can address the question as they choose to at home.

Working with families

Families are really involved in Head Start. In fact, they are required to spend a certain amount of time in the classroom. So I always have parents and guardians around when I'm teaching and there are lots of opportunities to talk. I also do home visits at all of the children's houses. I take that opportunity to ask a lot of questions about what the family celebrates, how they celebrate, and what holidays and rituals are important to them. Instead of just asking "What do you celebrate?" I ask, "What are the most important times of the year in your family? When do you get together? When do you get together with family members that live far away? Which holidays do you spend the most time preparing for? Which ones do you do the most cooking for?" I get rich information when I ask these questions.

Sometimes I also send out questionnaires that ask for similar information about holidays and how people celebrate. I work hard to make sure that the questionnaires get translated for families who speak languages other than English. If I can't find translators, I won't use a questionnaire, because I really want everyone to be included. I also follow up with families quite a few times to explain why I'm handing out the questionnaires and what I'm looking for. I want families to trust me so they feel comfortable sharing this special information with me.

When I want to include a classroom activity for a holiday celebrated by a particular family, I ask that family for a lot of input and guidance so I am sure to present it in an authentic, respectful way. For example, some of our families celebrate American New Year. For one family this was a particularly important holiday. I invited her in to share some of her rituals with the children. As a group we cooked black-eyed peas, because for her family, they are a symbol of good luck for the new year.

I feel lucky that families are so involved in Head Start. It makes my job easier, because families are right there to give input, act as resources, and share ideas. With their help, I'm able to implement holiday activities that build connections between home and school and represent individual families and their rituals and customs.

"Margery's Story"

Margery teaches kindergarten at St. Thomas School, a private, half-day kindergarten program which is a ministry of the Christian church that it is housed in. Its stated mission

Michael's, Sheryl's and Margery's Classrooms

lets it be known that St. Thomas is a Christian program with a Christian curriculum. St. Thomas is funded by family tuition and subsidization by the church.

The children who currently attend St. Thomas are Christian, mostly European American, and from middle-class families.

Approach to holidays

Holidays are a very important part of the program at St. Thomas. Holiday activities appear in the curriculum almost once a month, sometimes more. The administrators see holidays as a significant part of our Christian education curriculum component. Since we are in a Christian program, families are aware of this when they choose us for their children.

Goals

My goals with holidays are to model the Christian values that are important to us at St. Thomas, such as kindness, caring, forgiveness, compassion, honesty, responsibility, unity, peacefulness, respect, tolerance, and standing against injustice. Other goals are to teach the history of the Christian holidays, to help children learn more about each other, and to have fun. All of these goals are overall classroom goals too. The children and their families all really enjoy the holidays we celebrate.

Choosing holidays

The administration decides which holidays will be included in the curriculum. In general, we include all of the Christian holidays and a few non-sectarian holidays every year. The holidays are Thanksgiving, Advent, Christmas, New Year's, Martin Luther King, Jr.'s Birthday, Valentine's Day, St. Patrick's Day, Ash Wednesday, Good Friday, Easter, and the Fourth of July. We also talk a little bit about Palm Sunday and Holy Thursday as children bring them up. Many of our children attend church services on those days. We don't celebrate Halloween. The administrators and some of the families object to it because they feel it is anti-Christian. In my classroom, I also make mention of a few holidays of other religions as they are happening, so children know that there are other holidays and that people of different faiths observe them. I won't do any actual celebrating of those holidays, though. We also do Veterans Day as a "no war" day, because that holiday fits into St. Thomas' overall program goals of teaching nonviolence and peaceful problem solving.

Implementation

We do lots of holiday activities in the classroom, especially when I can demonstrate Christian values through them. Here are some examples of Christmas activities that we do in kindergarten. At meeting time we talk directly about what

Christmas is and why Christians observe it. I tell children that it is the time of the year when we celebrate the birth of baby Jesus. I explain that the reason we celebrate Jesus is because he modeled God's love. We talk about the Christmas story, specifically about Mary and Joseph going from inn to inn looking for a place to stay when Mary was about to give birth to Jesus. Children often want to talk about this story further, so I add wooden manger pieces to the block area that children can use to talk about, or even act out, the birth of baby Jesus. Some other activities I make available are those that focus on the giving as well as the receiving aspects of Christmas. There are materials for making Christmas ornaments and Christmas cards. I set up an activity area with boxes and wrapping paper, tape, and bows so children can "wrap" presents. Some children go from area to area and make something for their families or other people they care about. We have a wonderful Christmas family potluck one evening in December where we share food and then go out to carol for senior citizens. When we are finished singing, we come back to the school for hot chocolate. This is a real connecting time for families and children who all share a common religion and similar values and enjoy this community experience.

When we celebrate Thanksgiving we emphasize the underlying value of being thankful to God for all that God provides. We try to avoid the issue of "Pilgrims and Indians" because of all of the stereotypes in that story. We do lots of cooking and baking around that time of the year, though, and families come in quite a bit and share favorite family recipes. On the Wednesday before Thanksgiving, we invite all of the families in for a Harvest Feast, and we taste all of the fruits of our labor and enjoy spending time together.

Religion

At St. Thomas, we actively address the religious aspects of the holidays with the intent of teaching Christian values and beliefs. Many families choose to enroll their children at St. Thomas for this very reason. They are all supportive of this approach. In my kindergarten classroom I am careful to talk about God and Jesus in developmentally appropriate ways. We help children to see God in the awe and wonder of God's creations, such as the flowers, sunsets, and even worms. We also teach about God through the celebration of the children's lives and their relationships. In addition, we want them to experience God in their building of trust and being cared for in our program. This is how they know God. I am careful to allow children time to process information about God. They ask a lot of questions and I answer them simply and matter-of-factly. In all of this, I work with families so they are clear about what information their children are receiving and/or asking for. Then parents and guardians can support that curiosity at home in the ways they decide are best for them.

Celebrate!

Working with families

Parents are very involved at St. Thomas. Every year there is a "room parent" for each room who coordinates parties, fundraisers, and snacks for snack time. Other parents and guardians take turns bringing in and setting up for snacks. Families also really enjoy being involved in holiday activities at school. This is partly because holidays tend to be a big part of most of their own lives at home, and they enjoy sharing it with their children and with us. In my classroom, I regularly invite families to help with activities. Some families bring in cookies to share or a family recipe so we can make the cookies at school. Other families bring in decorations to put up in the classroom. Still others bring in holiday books to share with the children. I really encourage their participation, so they can model for children the fact that there are similarities and differences in the ways that all the families celebrate the same holidays. The families also help me coordinate our Christmas presentation, which we put on right before the winter break. They help make costumes, organize the potluck, and decorate the church basement.

Your holiday activities will not look exactly like any one of these programs. In fact, no two programs should look exactly alike, since no two programs have exactly the same make up of teachers, children, and families. You may find, however, that your holidays resemble bits and pieces of each of these three classrooms. That's fine. Use these descriptions to help you as you continue to refine your approach, your goals, and your work with families, and to carve out a holiday program that is just right for your setting.

A Final Word

Congratulations! You're now on your journey to creating a more meaningful, responsive holiday curriculum that reflects and meets the needs of the children and families in your program. Whether you have read this book from start to finish and begun to alter your approach to holidays, or just jumped around and read certain chapters, you have taken a positive step toward transforming an important part of your curriculum. Making change takes courage, strength, and a commitment to creating the best possible environment for the children in your care. Your efforts will play a valuable role in helping the children you care for to thrive in your program.

Resources

Books for Children

The following select list of books for children were included because they met the criteria of being accurate, sensitive, and reflective of the lives of real people; developmentally appropriate for young children; free of stereotypes; and, overall, good children's literature. Almost exclusively, the people and places in the books are set in present-day time. When the story happened some years ago, the pictures and experiences are familiar enough to children that they can relate to them.

Choose books for inclusion in your classroom that meet the criteria above and meet the needs of the particular children in your program. This means that books you choose should reflect the specific holidays that the children, families, and staff in your program celebrate, and how they celebrate them. They should help meet your program's holiday goals and follow your stated holiday policy. You may find that some books on this list meet those needs, others may not.

Keep in mind that there is not an equal balance of books about holidays available. There are many books based on some holidays, and few or none about others. Remember this as you look through this list. Also keep in mind that this is just a starting place, not a list of every available book. You might be able to find other books that will meet your needs by consulting Books in Print, available in many libraries. If you can't find a book you are looking for, consider making your own. That way you will be sure to represent equally the holidays that are important to the children and families in your program.

Birth Days and Rituals

Chocolate, Debbi. *On the Day I was Born.* New York, NY: Scholastic, Inc., 1995.

(Members of an extended African American family celebrate with joy and pride the birth of a firstborn son.)

Knight, Margy Burns. *Welcoming Babies.* Gardiner, ME: Tilbury House Publishers, 1994.

(A beautiful depiction of the welcoming celebrations of different cultures.)

Frasier, Debra. *On the Day You Were Born.* Orlando, FL: Harcourt Brace & Co., 1991.

(The earth celebrates the birth of a newborn baby.)

Roessel, Monty. *Kinaalda.* Minneapolis, MN: Lerner Publications Co., 1993.

(Celinda McKelvey, a Navajo girl, participates in the Kinaalda, the traditional coming-of-age ceremony of her people.)

Siegen-Smith, Nikki. *Welcome to the World: A Celebrations of Birth and Babies from Many Cultures.* New York, NY: Orchard, 1996.

(Beautiful photographs and poems.)

Columbus Day

Yolen, Jane. *Encounter.* New York, NY: Harcourt Brace Jovanovich, 1992.

(It is said that in 1492 Christopher Columbus discovered a new world, yet what he really found was a people with an established culture and civilization of their own. This is the story of that first meeting as seen through the eyes of a Taino boy.)

Rosh Hashanah

Goldin, Barbara Diamond. *The World's Birthday: A Rosh Hashanah Story.* New York, NY: Harcourt Brace & Co., 1990.

(Daniel is determined to have a birthday party for the world to celebrate Rosh Hashanah.)

Sukkot

Goldin, Barbara Diamond. *Night Lights: A Sukkot Story.* New York, NY: Harcourt Brace & Co., 1995.

(Daniel and his family build and prepare to celebrate and sleep in a *sukkah,* or hut, for the Jewish harvest festival, Sukkot.)

Halloween

Kroll, Steven. *The Biggest Pumpkin Ever*. New York, NY: Holiday House, 1984.

> (Two mice, each without the other's knowledge, help a pumpkin grow into "the biggest pumpkin ever"—but for different purposes.)

Titherington, Jeanne. *Pumpkin Pumpkin*. New York, NY: Mulberry Books, 1986.

> (Jamie plants a pumpkin seed, and after watching it grow, she carves the pumpkin and saves some seeds to plant in the spring.)

Diwali

Gilmore, Rachna. *Lights for Gita*. Gardiner, ME: Tillbury House, Publishers, 1994.

> (Recently immigrated from India, Gita is looking forward to celebrating her favorite holiday, Divali, a festival of lights, but thinks things are so different in her new home that she wonders if she will ever adjust.)

Deshpande, Chris. *Diwali*. London: A & C Black Publishers, 1994.

> (This story follows a group of children through the preparation and celebration of Diwali in school and at home.)

Dia de Los Muertos

Hoyt-Goldsmith, Diane. *Day of the Dead: A Mexican-American Celebration*. New York, NY: Holiday House, 1994.

> (A beautiful story that uses photographs of a contemporary Mexican American family to depict how they celebrate Dia de Los Muertos in their home.)

Lasky, Kathryn. *Days of the Dead*. New York, NY: Hyperion, 1994.

> (A story about how one family and their neighbors celebrate Los Dias de Los Muertos in a contemporary village in Mexico.)

Levy, Janice. *The Spirit of Tio Fernando/El espiritu de tio Fernando: A Day of the Dead Story*. Morton Grove, IL: Albert Whitman & Co.

> (As he prepares to celebrate the Day of the Dead, a young boy remembers all the things he liked about his favorite uncle. Bilingual in English and Spanish.)

Thanksgiving/Being Thankful (See also Seasonal/Harvest)

Bunting, Eve. *How Many Days to America? A Thanksgiving Story*. New York, NY: Clarion Books, 1988.

> (Refugees from a Caribbean island embark on a dangerous boat trip to America where they have a special reason to celebrate Thanksgiving.)

Swamp, Chief Jake. *Giving Thanks: A Native American Good Morning Message*. New York, NY: Lee & Low Books, Inc., 1995.

> (Mohawk parents have traditionally taught their children to start each day by giving thanks to Mother Earth. Known as the Thanksgiving Address, this good morning message has been adapted by Chief Jake Swamp of the Mohawk Nation especially for readers of all ages. Simple language and beautiful, colorful pictures.)

Solstice

Jackson, Ellen. *The Winter Solstice*. Brookfield, CT: The Millbrook Press, 1994.

> (Presents facts and folklore about the shortest day of the year; a day that has been filled with magic since ancient times.)

George, Jean Craighead. *Dear Rebecca, Winter is Here*. New York, NY: HarperCollins, 1993.

> (A grandmother explains to her granddaughter how the arrival of winter brings changes in nature and the earth's creatures.)

Hanukkah

Behrens, June. *Hanukkah*. Chicago, IL: Children's Press, 1983.

> (The story of Hanukkah and how one family celebrates it.)

Kuskin, Karla. *A Great Miracle Happened There*. New York, NY: HarperTrophy, 1993.

> (On the first night of Hanukkah, a mother tells her family and a young guest the story of the holiday's origin.)

Gellman, Ellie. *Jeremy's Dreidel*. Rockville, MD: Kar-Ben Copies, Inc., 1992.

> (Jeremy signs up for a Hanukkah workshop to make unusual dreidels and creates a clay dreidel with braille dots for his dad, who is blind.)

Drucker, Malka. *Grandma's Latkes*. New York, NY: Harcourt Brace & Co., 1992.

> (Every year Grandma prepares the latkes for the family's Hanukkah meal, following the recipe handed down by her grandmother. This year Molly is finally old enough to help, and to learn Grandma's secrets.)

Adler, David. *One Yellow Daffodil: A Hanukkah Story*. New York, NY: Harcourt Brace & Co., 1995.

> (During Hanukkah two children help a Holocaust survivor to once again embrace his religious traditions.)

Christmas

Bunting, Eve. *The Night Tree*. New York, NY: Harcourt Brace & Co., 1991.

> (The story of one family's Christmas Eve tradition of decorating a tree in the woods with edible treats for forest animals to enjoy.)

Thomas, Jane Resh. *Lights on the River*. New York, NY: Hyperion Books for Children, 1994.

> (The story of a young daughter of migrant farm workers who longs for Christmas and her Abuela in Mexico.)

Soto, Gary. *Too Many Tamales*. New York, NY: G. P. Putnam's Sons, 1993.

> (Maria tries on her mother's wedding ring while helping make tamales for a Christmas family get-together. Panic ensues when, hours later, she realizes the ring is missing.)

Brown, Margery Wheeler. *Baby Jesus Like My Brother*. East Orange, NJ: Just Us Books, 1995.

> (On a bright, starry night, the night before Christmas, Tony's big sister, Keisha, explains that Christmas is Jesus' birthday. And that Jesus' parents tried to do as much as they could for the new baby—just as Keisha and Tony's parents do for their new baby brother.)

Christmas and Hanukkah

Moorman, Margaret. *Light the Lights!* New York, NY: Scholastic, Inc., 1994.

> (A story of a family who celebrates both Christmas and Hanukkah.)

Kwanzaa

Burden-Patmon, Denise. *Imani's Gift at Kwanzaa*. New York, NY: Simon & Schuster, 1992.

> (Imani reflects on the meaning of Kwanzaa while her family celebrates this cultural event.)

Chocolate, Deborah M. Newton. *Kwanzaa*. Chicago, IL: Children's Press, 1990.

> (A beautiful story of how one family celebrates Kwanzaa. Includes information about the meaning of the Nguzo Saba, the Seven Principles of Kwanzaa.)

Chocolate, Deborah M. Newton. *My First Kwanzaa Book*. New York: Scholastic, Inc., 1992.

> (In simple text and colorful pictures, this story introduces young children to the joyous celebration of Kwanzaa.)

Chinese New Year

Waters, Kate and Slovenz-Low, Madeline. *Lion Dancer: Ernie Wan's Chinese New Year*. New York: Scholastic, Inc., 1990.

> (This is the story of the most important day of Ernie Wan's life. This Chinese New Year he will perform his first Lion Dance on the streets of New York City!)

Chinn, Karen. *Sam and the Lucky Money*. New York, NY: Lee & Low Books, Inc., 1995.

> (Sam must decide how to spend the lucky money he's received for Chinese New Year.)

Brown, Tricia. *Chinese New Year*. New York, NY: Henry Holt & Co., 1987.

> (The text and photographs depict the celebration of Chinese New Year by Chinese Americans living in San Francisco.)

Martin Luther King, Jr.'s Birthday

Green, Carol. *Martin Luther King, Jr.: A Man Who Changed Things*. Chicago, IL: Children's Press, 1989.

> (A beautiful book with real photographs of Martin Luther King, Jr., Coretta Scott King, Rosa Parks, and others that tells the story of Martin Luther King, Jr., and others who struggled for peace and justice.)

Boone-Jones, Margaret. *Martin Luther King, Jr.: A Picture Story*. Chicago, IL: Children's Press, 1968.

> (The story of young Martin Luther King, Jr.'s life and how he became involved in social justice work.)

Têt

Tran, Kim-Lan. *Têt: The New Year*. New York, NY: Simon & Schuster, 1992.

> (Huy and his father, who recently immigrated to the U.S. from Viet Nam, join Huy's teachers and classmates at their teacher's apartment for a Têt celebration.)

Valentine's Day

Sabuda, Robert. *Saint Valentine*. New York, NY: Simon & Schuster, 1992.

> (Recounts an incident in the life of Saint Valentine, a physician who lived some 200 years after Christ, in which he treated a small child for blindness, and was later imprisoned. Includes historical perspectives on the meaning of present-day Valentine's Day.)

Purim

Wolkstein, Diane. *Esther's Story*. New York, NY: Morrow Junior Books, 1996.

> (This story of Esther reveals the transformation of a shy little girl into a compassionate queen who is willing to risk the wrath of a king in order to save her people.)

Kahn, Katherine Janus. *The Purim Parade*. Rockville, MD: Kar-Ben Copies, Inc., 1986.

> (This toddler-size board book depicts the dressing-up and Purim parade that many young children enjoy during this holiday.)

Nerlove, Miriam. *Purim*. Morton Grove, IL: Albert Whitman & Co., 1992.

> (A young boy becomes caught up in the excitement of the Purim celebration as the rabbi relates the tale of the courageous Queen Esther and the evil Haman.)

St. Patrick's Day

Kroll, Steven. *Mary McLean and the St. Patrick's Day Parade*. New York, NY: Scholastic, Inc., 1991.

> (Mary wanted more than anything to ride with Mr. Finnegan in the St. Patrick's Day parade. He agreed, if she could bring him a perfect shamrock.)

Easter

Gibbons, Gail. *Easter*. New York, NY: Holiday House, 1989.

> (With simple text and colorful pictures, this book examines the background, significance, symbols, and traditions of Easter.)

Polacco, Patricia. *Rechenka's Eggs*. New York, NY: Putnam & Grosset Group, 1988.

> (An injured goose rescued by Babushka, having broken the painted eggs intended for the Easter Festival in Moscva, lays thirteen marvelously colored eggs to replace them, then leaves behind one final miracle in egg form before returning to her own kind.)

Fisher, Aileen. *The Story of Easter*. New York, NY: HarperCollins, 1997.

> (Presents the background and significance of the Christian celebration of Easter.)

Passover

Hannigan, Lynne. *Sam's Passover*. London: A & C Black Publishers, 1995.

> (Sam and his family have a special meal at home to remember the story of Passover. At school, Sam's class goes to the synagogue to find out about the story.)

Krulik, Nancy. *Penny and the Four Questions*. New York, NY: Scholastic, Inc., 1993.

> (A special story of friendship and a little girl who learns the true meaning of Passover.)

Polacco, Patricia. *Mrs. Katz and Tush*. New York, NY: Bantam Doubleday, 1992.

> (Larnel and Mrs. Katz become friends when Larnel agrees to help care for Mrs. Katz's new cat, Tush. As Larnel grows to love Mrs. Katz, he also learns about the suffering and triumph black history shares with the Jewish heritage. Finally, they celebrate a festive Passover seder together.)

Cinco de Mayo

Behrens, June. *Fiesta: Cinco de Mayo*. Chicago, IL: Children's Press, 1978.

> (A story of a contemporary Cinco de Mayo fiesta. Actual photographs.)

Kodomo-no-hi (Japanese Children's Day)

Kroll, Virginia. *A Carp for Kimiko*. Watertown, MA: Charlesbridge Publishing, 1993.

> (Although the tradition is to present carp kites only to boys on Children's Day, Kimiko's parents find a way to make the day special for her.)

Ramadan

Ghazi, Suhaib Hamid. *Ramadan*. New York, NY: Holiday House, 1996.

> (Describes the celebration of the month of Ramadan by an Islamic family and discusses the meaning and importance of this holiday in the Islamic religion.)

Matthews, Mary. *Magid Fasts for Ramadan*. New York, NY: Clarion Books, 1996.

> (Magid, an eight-year-old Muslim boy in Cairo, is determined to celebrate Ramadan by fasting, despite the opposition of family members who feel that he is not yet old enough to fast.)

El-Moslimany, Ann. *Zaki's Ramadhan Fast*. Seattle, WA: Amica Publishing House, 1994.

> (Even though he is not required to fast during this special month of Ramadhan, Zaki's mother, father, and sister give him their support to achieve his goal of fasting for one day.)

Id ul-Fitr

Stone, Susheila. *Eid ul-Fitr*. London: A & C Black Publishers, 1994.

> (This story follows a young girl as she celebrates Id ul-Fitr, the three-day festival at the end of Ramadan, both at home and at school.)

Potlatch

Hoyt-Goldsmith, Diane. *Potlatch: A Tsimshian Celebration*. New York, NY: Holiday House, 1997.

> (Describes the traditions of the Tsimshian Indians living in Metlakatla, Alaska, and in particular, those connected with a potlatch they hold to celebrate their heritage. Beautiful, contemporary photographs.)

Powwow

Ancona, George, *Powwow*. New York, NY: Harcourt Brace & Co., 1993.

> (A photo essay on the pan-Indian celebration called a powwow, this particular one being held on the Crow Reservation in Montana.)

Behrens, June. *Powwow*. Chicago, IL: Children's Press, 1983.

> (Describes a visit to a powwow where American Indian families get together to enjoy traditional food, music, dancing, and crafts.)

Seasonal/Harvest

Hoyt-Goldsmith, Diane. *Cherokee Summer*. New York, NY: Holiday House, 1993.

> (This story about Bridget, a young Cherokee Indian girl, and her family includes information about and history of the Cherokee people, Cherokee traditions, and a Summer Stomp Dance. Beautiful, contemporary photographs.)

Hutchings, Amy and Richard. *Picking Apples & Pumpkins*. New York, NY: Scholastic, Inc., 1994.

> (A story of a family and some friends who go to a pumpkin patch to pick out pumpkins and go to an apple orchard to pick apples for apple pie.)

Ray, Mary Lyn. *Pumpkins*. New York, NY: Harcourt Brace & Co., 1992.

> (A man harvests and sells a bountiful crop of pumpkins so that he will be able to preserve a field from developers. A great activism book.)

Regguinti, Gordon. *The Sacred Harvest: Ojibway Wild Rice Gathering*. Minneapolis, MN: Lerner Publications Co., 1992.

> (Glen Jackson, Jr., an eleven-year-old Ojibway Indian in northern Minnesota, goes with his father to harvest wild rice, the sacred food of his people.)

Peters, Russel M. *Clambake: A Wampanoag Tradition*. Minneapolis, MN: Lerner Publications Co., 1992.

> (Steven Peters, a Wampanoag Indian in Massachusetts, learns from his grandfather how to prepare a clambake in the tradition of his people. Beautiful, contemporary photographs.)

Wittstock, Laura Waterman. *Inintag's Gift of Sugar: Traditional Native Sugarmaking*. Minneapolis, MN: Lerner Publications Co., 1993.

> (Describes how Native Americans have relied on the sugar maple tree for food and tells how an Anishinabe Indian in Minnesota continues his people's traditions by teaching students to tap the trees and make maple sugar.)

General/Compilations

Baylor, Byrd. *I'm in Charge of Celebrations*. New York, NY: Charles Scribner's Sons, 1986.

> (A young girl makes up her own celebrations that honor the wilderness.)

Livingston, Myra Cohn. *Festivals*. New York: Holiday House, 1996.

> (Poems celebrating fourteen festivals including Chinese New Year, Kwanzaa, Purim, Ramadan, Mardi Gras, and Now-Ruz.)

Ancona, George. *The Piñata Maker/El Pinatero*. Orlando, FL: Harcourt Brace & Co., 1994.

> (Describes how Don Ricardo, a craftsman from Ejutia de Crespo in southern Mexico, makes piñatas for all the village birthday parties and other fiestas. Bilingual with real photographs of contemporary life in a Mexican village.)

Blue, Rose. *Good Yontif: A Picture Book of the Jewish Year*. Brookfield, CT: The Millbrook Press, 1997.

> (Information about the various Jewish holy days throughout the year follows a series of illustrations showing a young boy and his family celebrating each holiday.)

Viesti, Joe and Hall, Diane. *Celebrate! In Southeast Asia*. New York, NY: Lothrop, Lee & Shepard Books, 1996.

> (Describes a variety of holiday celebrations in Southeast Asia, including Thailand's Elephant Round-Up, Singapore's Moon Cake Festival, and the Vietnamese New Year.)

Viesti, Joe and Hall, Diane. *Celebrate! In South Asia*. New York, NY: Lothrop, Lee & Shepard Books, 1996.

> (Describes religious festivals and sacred days in India, Sri Lanka, Bangladesh, Pakistan, Bhutan, Burma, and Nepal.)

Celebrate!

Books About Similarities and Differences

Cheltenham Elementary School Kindergartens. *We Are All Alike . . . We Are All Different.* New York, NY: Scholastic, Inc., 1991.

Dooley, Norah. *Everybody Cooks Rice.* New York, NY: Scholastic, Inc., 1991.

Intrater, Roberta Grobel. *Two Eyes, A Nose, and A Mouth.* New York, NY: Scholastic, Inc., 1995.

Kroll, Virginia. *Hats off to Hair!* Watertown, MA: Charlesbridge Publishing, 1995.

Simon, Norma. *Why Am I Different?* Morton Grove, IL: Albert Whitman & Co., 1976.

Adult Resources

Books

Holidays

Berg, Elizabeth. *Family Traditions: Celebrations for Holidays and Everyday.* Pleasantville, NY: The Reader's Digest Association, Inc., 1992.

Bisson, Julie. *Celebrating Holidays in the Anti-Bias Early Childhood Education Program.* Pasadena, CA: Pacific Oaks Unpublished Masters Thesis, 1992. (A summarized version of a part of this thesis is available for a nominal charge from Pacific Oaks College Bookstore, 5 Westmoreland Place, Pasadena, CA 91103.)

Booze, Regena. *Incorporating the Principles of Kwanzaa into your Daily Curriculum: A Handbook for Teachers of Young Children.* Pasadena, CA: Pacific Oaks Unpublished Masters Thesis, 1988.

Creaser, Barbara and Dau, Elizabeth. *Who's in Charge of Celebrations? A Child-Centered Approach.* AECA Resource Book Series, Australian Early Childhood Association, P.O. Box 105, Watson ACT 2606, 1994.

Darian, Shea. *Seven Times the Sun: Guiding Your Child Through the Rhythms of the Day.* San Diego, CA: LuraMedia, 1994.

Imber-Black, Evan and Roberts, Janine. *Rituals for Our Times: Celebrating, Healing, and Changing Our Lives and Our Relationships.* New York, NY: HarperCollins Publishers, Inc., 1992.

Leiberman, Susan Abel. *New Traditions: Redefining Celebrations for Today's Family.* New York, NY: Noonday Press, 1991.

Macgregor, Cynthia. *Family Customs & Traditions.* Minneapolis, MN: Fairview Press, 1995.

Robinson, Jo and Coppock Staeheli, Jean. *Unplug the Christmas Machine.* New York, NY: William Morrow, 1991.

Santino, Jack. *All Around the Year: Holidays and Celebrations in American Life.* Chicago, IL: University of Illinois Press, 1995.

Stone, Jane Davis. *A Jehovah's Witness Perspective on Holiday Curriculum.* Pasadena, CA: Pacific Oaks Unpublished Masters Thesis, 1991.

General Education

Bredekamp, Sue and Copple, Carol (Eds.). *Developmentally Appropriate Practice in Early Childhood Programs, Revised Edition.* Washington, D.C.: NAEYC, 1997.

Carter, Margie and Curtis, Deb. *Training Teachers: A Harvest of Theory and Practice.* St. Paul, MN: Redleaf Press, 1994.

DeGaetano, Gloria & Arnold, Maureen. *Media Smarts 4 Young Folks.* Los Angeles, CA: Merrie Way CommUnity, 1997.

Levin, Diane and Carlsson-Paige, Nancy. *Who's Calling the Shots? How to Respond Effectively to Children's Fascination with War Play and War Toys.* Philadelphia, PA: New Society Publishers, 1990.

Zinn, Howard. *A People's History of the United States: 1492 to Present, Revised and Updated.* New York, NY: HarperCollins, 1995.

Anti-Bias/Multicultural

Delpit, Lisa. *Other People's Children: Cultural Conflict in the Classroom.* New York, NY: The New Press, 1995.

Derman-Sparks, Louise and the ABC Task Force. *Anti-Bias Curriculum: Tools for Empowering Young Children.* Washington, DC: NAEYC, 1989.

Gonzalez-Mena, Janet. *Multicultural Issues in Child Care.* Mountain View, CA: Mayfield Publishing Company, 1993.

Kendall, Frances E. *Diversity in the Classroom: New Approaches to the Education of Young Children, Second Edition.* New York, NY: Teacher's College Press, 1996.

Ladson-Billings, Gloria. *The Dreamkeepers: Successful Teachers of African American Children.* San Francisco, CA: Jossey-Bass Publishers, 1994.

Ramsey, Patricia. *Teaching and Learning in a Diverse World.* New York, NY: Teacher's College Press, 1987.

Slapin, Beverly and Seale, Doris. *Through Indian Eyes: The Native Experience in Books for Children.* Philadelphia, PA: New Society Publishers, 1987.

Williams, Leslie & De Gaetano, Yvonne. *Alerta: A Multicultural, Bilingual Approach to Teaching Young Children.* Menlo Park, CA: Addison-Wesley Publishing Company, 1985.

York, Stacey. *Roots and Wings: Affirming Culture in Early Childhood Programs.* St. Paul, MN: Redleaf Press, 1991.

Religion

Fay, Martha. *Children and Religion: Making Choices in a Secular Age.* New York, NY: Fireside, 1993.

Ganeri, Anita. *Religions Explained: A Beginner's Guide to World Faiths.* New York, NY: Henry Holt & Co., 1997.

Heller, David. *Talking to Your Child About God: A Book for Families of All Faiths.* New York, NY: Bantam, 1990.

Westerhoff, John H. *Will Our Children Have Faith?* New York, NY: Seabury, 1976.

Articles

Westerhoff, John H. "Celebrating Holidays in Early Childhood Programs." *The Academy Update,* NAEYC (Winter 1996): 4–5.

———. "Celebrate Holidays and Diversity." *Early Childhood Today* (1994): 44–52.

———. "Beginnings Workshop." *Child Care Information Exchange* (November/December 1994): 39–58.

Brunson Phillips, Carol. "Nurturing Diversity for Today's Children and Tomorrow's Leaders." *Young Children* (1988): 42–47.

Cox, Meg. "The Rewards of Rituals." *Parents* (November 1995): 116–119.

Darian, Shea. "The Gift of Our Presence: Honoring Children on their Birthdays." *Mothering* (Fall 1996): 33–35.

Dimidjian, Victoria Jean. "Holidays, Holy Days, and Wholly Dazed: Approaches to Special Days." *Young Children* (September 1989): 70–75.

Dorris, Michael. "Why I'm Not Thankful for Thanksgiving." *Interracial Books for Children Bulletin* (1978): 6–9.

Evans, Debbie. "I Won't Lie About Santa." *Parents* (December 1996): 32.

Gelb, Steven. "Christmas Programming in Schools: Unintended Consequences." *Childhood Education* (1987): 9–13.

Ramsey, Patricia. "Beyond Ten Little Indians and Turkeys." *Young Children* (September 1989): 28–51.

Root, Susan. "A Party for Me." *First Teacher* (November/December 1995): 26–27.

Stephens, Karen. "Preventing the Holiday Crazies." *First Teacher* (November/December 1995): 8–9.

Wardle, Francis. "Bunny Ears and Cupcakes for All: Are Parties Developmentally Appropriate?" *Child Care Information Exchange* (1990): 39–41.

Watch Tower Bible and Tract Society of Pennsylvania. "School and Jehovah's Witnesses." New York, NY: Watch Tower Bible and Tract Society of New York, Inc., 1983.

Resources

Other Resources from Redleaf Press

ALL THE COLORS WE ARE: THE STORY OF HOW WE GET OUR SKIN COLOR

by Katie Kissinger

Selected by Parent Council for its photographs and engaging language, *All the Colors We Are* helps children understand the truths about skin color and that it is one way we are special and different from one another. Includes unique activity ideas. Bilingual English/Spanish.

ROOTS AND WINGS: AFFIRMING CULTURE IN EARLY CHILDHOOD PROGRAMS, REVISED EDITION

by Stacey York

With over 100 new and revised activities, practical examples, and staff-training recommendations, this revised edition of the bestselling *Roots and Wings* also includes new chapters on bilingual education, culturally responsive teaching, and children and prejudice.

MAKING IT BETTER: ACTIVITIES FOR LIVING IN A STRESSFUL WORLD

by Barbara Oehlberg

More than 70 activities give caregivers the confidence to help children survive, thrive, and learn by engaging children in self-healing, empathy, and empowerment.

FOR THE LOVE OF CHILDREN: DAILY AFFIRMATIONS FOR PEOPLE WHO CARE FOR CHILDREN

by Jean Steiner and Mary Steiner Whelan

An empowering book filled with quotations, stories, and affirmations for each day of the year. Here is the perfect gift for everyone who cares for children, infant through school age.

REFLECTING CHILDREN'S LIVES: A HANDBOOK FOR PLANNING CHILD-CENTERED CURRICULUM

by Deb Curtis and Margie Carter

Rethink your ideas about scheduling, observation, play, materials, space, and emergent themes with these original approaches. Lots of classroom examples and ideas to spark your creativity.

THE KINDNESS CURRICULUM: INTRODUCING YOUNG CHILDREN TO LOVING VALUES

by Judith Anne Rice

Create opportunities for kids to practice kindness, empathy, conflict resolution, and respect using more than 60 imaginative, exuberant activities that are invaluable when instilling character and kindness. Includes activity sheets for parents and children to do at home.

SO THIS IS NORMAL TOO? TEACHERS AND PARENTS WORKING OUT DEVELOPMENTAL ISSUES IN YOUNG CHILDREN

by Deborah Hewitt

This guide makes the challenging behaviors of children a vehicle for cooperation among adults and stepping stones to learning for children.

800-423-8309
www.redleafpress.org